英语3知识点强化练习

主 编 徐昌华 李泽佳 于小华
副主编 闫秀慧 孙美杰 薛鸿燕 范复旺

北京理工大学出版社
BEIJING INSTITUTE OF TECHNOLOGY PRESS

版权专有　侵权必究

图书在版编目(CIP)数据

英语 3 知识点强化练习 / 徐昌华，李泽佳，于小华主编. -- 北京：北京理工大学出版社，2023.5
ISBN 978-7-5763-2424-2

Ⅰ.①英… Ⅱ.①徐… ②李… ③于… Ⅲ.①英语课-中等专业学校-升学参考资料 Ⅳ.①G634.413

中国国家版本馆 CIP 数据核字(2023)第 096699 号

出版发行 / 北京理工大学出版社有限责任公司
社　　址 / 北京市海淀区中关村南大街 5 号
邮　　编 / 100081
电　　话 / (010)68914775(总编室)
　　　　　 (010)82562903(教材售后服务热线)
　　　　　 (010)68944723(其他图书服务热线)
网　　址 / http://www.bitpress.com.cn
经　　销 / 全国各地新华书店
印　　刷 / 定州市新华印刷有限公司
开　　本 / 787 毫米×1092 毫米　1/16
印　　张 / 11　　　　　　　　　　　　　责任编辑 / 王晓莉
字　　数 / 233 千字　　　　　　　　　　文案编辑 / 王晓莉
版　　次 / 2023 年 5 月第 1 版　2023 年 5 月第 1 次印刷　责任校对 / 周瑞红
定　　价 / 35.00 元　　　　　　　　　　责任印制 / 边心超

图书出现印装质量问题，请拨打售后服务热线，本社负责调换

前 言

本书依据《中等职业学校英语课程标准（2020年版）》，结合中等职业学校就业与升学的实际情况而编写。

本书能够夯实学生的英语学习基础，适用于所有中职学生的英语学习。共分为8个单元，每个单元所附的习题，以Warming-up、Listening and Speaking、Reading and Writing、Grammar以及For Better Performance五个模块的形式展开，呈现方式多样化，以语音、填空、选择、对话练习、完形填空、阅读理解、改错及写作的练习方式帮助学生掌握词汇、课文内容和语法知识，使其拓展知识面，提高英语水平。针对学生高考的需求，在每个单元的学习内容结束后，本书又附有单元检测习题，习题内容符合对口英语高考大纲，且题型与高考题型一致，能有效地达到举一反三、灵活运用所学知识点的目的，可以帮助学生在日常学习中巩固基础、提高技能。本书很好地满足了职业学校的学生参加职教高考的需求。

我们本着"注重基础，突出运用，精选内容，强化训练，提高分数"的原则，力争做到"由浅入深、循序渐进"，符合中等职业学校学生的认知特点和接受能力。本书可作为中等职业学校教师的复习教学用书，也可作为一、二年级学生日常学习用书，而对于参加对口升学的毕业班学生来说，其同样适用。

本书的作者均是来自教学一线、有多年教学经验的教师。但由于水平有限，疏漏与不足之处在所难免，恳请各位老师、同学及其他读者批评指正。

编　者

目 录

Unit 1 Festivals Around the World ·· 1
    Warming-up ·· 1
    Listening and Speaking ·· 2
    Reading and Writing ·· 3
    Grammar ·· 5
    For Better Performance ·· 8
    单元检测 ·· 10

Unit 2 Community Life ··· 18
    Warming-up ·· 18
    Listening and Speaking ·· 19
    Reading and Writing ·· 21
    Grammar ·· 23
    For Better Performance ··· 26
    单元检测 ·· 27

Unit 3 Artificial Intelligence ·· 36
    Warming-up ·· 36
    Listening and Speaking ·· 37
    Reading and Writing ·· 38
    Grammar ·· 41
    For Better Performance ··· 44
    单元检测 ·· 45

Unit 4 Customer Service ·· 54
    Warming-up ·· 54
    Listening and Speaking ·· 55
    Reading and Writing ·· 57
    Grammar ·· 59
    For Better Performance ··· 62
    单元检测 ·· 63

英语3知识点强化练习

Unit 5　Natural Wonders in the World ·················· 73
    Warming-up ·················· 73
    Listening and Speaking ·················· 74
    Reading and Writing ·················· 75
    Grammar ·················· 78
    For Better Performance ·················· 81
    单元检测 ·················· 82

Unit 6　Living History of Culture ·················· 91
    Warming-up ·················· 91
    Listening and Speaking ·················· 92
    Reading and Writing ·················· 94
    Grammar ·················· 96
    For Better Performance ·················· 99
    单元检测 ·················· 101

Unit 7　Natural Disasters ·················· 110
    Warming-up ·················· 110
    Listening and Speaking ·················· 111
    Reading and Writing ·················· 112
    Grammar ·················· 115
    For Better Performance ·················· 118
    单元检测 ·················· 119

Unit 8　Role Models of the Times ·················· 128
    Warming-up ·················· 128
    Listening and Speaking ·················· 129
    Reading and Writing ·················· 130
    Grammar ·················· 133
    For Better Performance ·················· 136
    单元检测 ·················· 137

Unit 1

Festivals Around the World

Warming-up

一、句型汇总

1. The typical tradition is eating moon cakes. 典型的传统是吃月饼。

2. People splash water at one another as a sign of happiness and good luck for the coming year.
人们互相泼水,作为来年幸福和好运的象征。

3. Dragon boat racing is a popular activity. 赛龙舟是一项很受欢迎的活动。

4. Family members get together and enjoy a big dinner. 家庭成员聚在一起享受一顿丰盛的晚餐。

5. It's a reunion time for families and friends. 这是家人和朋友团聚的时刻。

6. The Spring Festival marks the beginning of the Chinese Lunar New Year. 春节标志着中国农历新年的开始。

7. People prefer going to the temple fairs to buy traditional crafts. 人们更喜欢去庙会买传统工艺品。

8. Children knock on the door for treat of sweets or snacks. 孩子们敲门要糖果或零食。

9. People splash water at each other in a playful manner. 人们以一种戏谑的方式向对方泼水。

二、英汉互译

1. appreciate _____
2. symbol _____
3. performance _____
4. decorate _____
5. fireplace _____
6. 收到 _____
7. 打闹的 _____
8. 手艺 _____
9. 庆典 _____
10. 团圆 _____

Listening and Speaking

一、找出与所给单词画线部分读音相同的选项

(　　) 1. exp<u>e</u>ct　　A. <u>e</u>xpress　　B. <u>e</u>xcellent　　C. <u>e</u>xit　　D. <u>e</u>xercise

(　　) 2. cr<u>a</u>ft　　A. ch<u>a</u>racter　　B. <u>a</u>gree　　C. <u>a</u>dvice　　D. f<u>a</u>st

(　　) 3. now<u>a</u>days　　A. f<u>a</u>rewell　　B. <u>a</u>fford　　C. b<u>a</u>ggage　　D. ch<u>a</u>mpion

(　　) 4. sn<u>a</u>ck　　A. n<u>a</u>rrow　　B. l<u>a</u>st　　C. s<u>a</u>me　　D. g<u>a</u>la

(　　) 5. tr<u>a</u>ditional　　A. w<u>a</u>steland　　B. <u>a</u>ppreciate　　C. decor<u>a</u>te　　D. firepl<u>a</u>ce

二、从 B 栏中找出与 A 栏中相对应的答语

A
1. When is the Spring Festival?
2. How do you celebrate the festival?
3. What festival are you going to celebrate?
4. Do you want to celebrate together?
5. Would you like to come?

B
A. Of course!
B. The Spring Festival.
C. It falls on the 1st day of the first Chinese Lunar month.
D. By enjoying the big reunion dinner.
E. Yes, I do.

三、用所给句子补全下面对话

A: Hello, Mary. I plan to celebrate the Spring Festival with my family. ___1___

B: I'd love to, I've never been to a Chinese festival before! ___2___

A: It falls on the 1st day of the first Chinese lunar month. The Spring Festival marks the beginning of the Chinese Lunar New Year.

Unit 1　Festivals Around the World

B：__3__ So how do you celebrate it?

A：We will have a reunion dinner together and watch the Spring Festival Gala.

B：__4__ Thank you for your invitation!

A：That's all right. __5__

B：Me too.

> A. I hope you will have an unforgettable experience.
> B. Do you want to celebrate together?
> C. When is the Spring Festival?
> D. Sounds similar to Christmas in my country.
> E. That's so nice!

四、场景模拟

编写一组对话,向你的外国朋友 Emily 介绍一个中国的传统节日。

提示词汇：the beginning of/firework/similar to

Reading and Writing

一、用单词的适当形式填空

1. We will have a reunion dinner together and watch the Spring Festival _____ (庆典).

2. Sounds _____ (相似) to Christmas in my country.

3. _____ (现今), the world is developing rapidly.

4. It was a wonderful _____ (表演).

5. Dragon boat _____ (race) is a popular activity.

6. Children knock on the door for treat of sweets or _____ (snack).

7. People splash water at one another as a _____ (标志) of happiness and good luck for the coming year.

8. People prefer going to the temple fairs to buy traditional _____ (craft).

9. Every cadre who thinks for the people deserves our _____ (respect).

10. How do you like this _____ (decorate)?

二、完形填空

The fourth Thursday in November is called Thanksgiving Day. __1__ this day, families and

— 3 —

friends get together, __2__ a meal and give thanks for the blessings of good health, food, jobs, and families.

In 1620, a group of Pilgrims(清教徒) left from England to search for __3__ freedom, part of whom were Protestants(新教徒). And they __4__ to America on a small sailboat named the Mayflower finally. And they __5__ at what is now Plymouth, Massachusetts(普利茅斯,马萨诸塞州), in icy November. The price in human lives and tragedy had been great. __6__ the other hand, they saw new hope for the future. The first __7__ Thanksgiving in America took place in Plymouth colony(殖民地), Massachusetts in October 1621. Thanksgiving did not become a national holiday __8__ 1863 during the American Civil War. In the United States, thanksgiving dinner is practically the same all over the country. The table is always loaded with delicious food of many different kinds. Naturally, the main course is turkey (a bird __9__ to the Americans), with an array of vegetables and desserts. Pumpkin pie is often served in remembrance __10__ the first settlers.

( ) 1. A. For   B. On   C. From   D. By
( ) 2. A. shape   B. share   C. shame   D. shave
( ) 3. A. religion   B. region   C. religious   D. regional
( ) 4. A. shipped   B. boated   C. swam   D. sailed
( ) 5. A. landed   B. reached   C. got   D. settled
( ) 6. A. At   B. By   C. On   D. In
( ) 7. A. official   B. office   C. government   D. unofficial
( ) 8. A. in   B. until   C. till   D. after
( ) 9. A. born   B. live   C. native   D. natural
( ) 10. A. with   B. for   C. to   D. of

三、阅读理解

阅读下面短文,从每题所给的 A、B、C、D 四个选项中选出最佳答案。

Dragon Boat Festival, often known as Duan Wu Festival, is a traditional Chinese festival held on the fifth day of the fifth month of the Chinese calendar. It is also known as the Double Fifth. It has been celebrated, in various ways, in other parts of East Asia as well, most notably Korea.

The exact origins of Duan Wu are unclear, but one traditional view holds that the festival memorializes the Chinese poet Qu Yuan of the Warring States Period. He committed suicide by drowning himself in a river because he was disgusted by the corruption of the Chu government. The local people, knowing him to be a good man, decided to throw food into the river to feed the fishes to _____ them from eating Qu's body. They also sat on dragon boats, and

Unit 1　Festivals Around the World

tried to scare the fishes away by the thundering sound of drums aboard the boat and the fierce-looking dragon-head in the front of the boat.

　　In the early years of the Chinese Republic, Duan Wu was also celebrated as "Poets' Day", due to Qu Yuan's status as China's first poet of personal renown.

　　Today, people eat *zongzi* and race dragon boats in memory of Qu's dramatic death.

(　　)1. When is the Dragon Boat Festival?
　　A. The fifth day of the second month.　B. The fifth day of the fifth month.
　　C. The fifth day of the first month.　　D. Unclear.

(　　)2. The Dragon Boat Festival is also called _____ in the article.
　　A. Duan Wu Festival　　　　　　　　B. The Double Fourth
　　C. The article doesn't say　　　　　　D. Qu Yuan Memorial Day

(　　)3. Which of the following can be put in "_____" in the second paragraph?
　　A. prevent　　B. impel　　C. out　　D. refrain

(　　)4. Duan Wu was also celebrated as "Poets' Day", due to _____ status as China's first poet of personal renown.
　　A. Qu Yuan's　B. God's　　C. Qu's　　D. someone's

(　　)5. What do people do now to commemorate Qu Yuan?
　　A. Set off fireworks.　　　　　　　　B. Write poems.
　　C. Eat *zongzi* and race dragon boats.　D. Do nothing.

四、书面表达

以"The Mid-Autumn Festival"为题，写一篇文章，字数80～100字。

_____
_____
_____
_____

Grammar

一、从下面每小题四个选项中选出最佳选项

(　　)1. People in Guangzhou like _____ the line dance.

A. watch   B. watches   C. watching   D. watched

( ) 2. The reporter didn't go to bed until he finished _____ the article.

A. writing   B. write   C. to write   D. wrote

( ) 3. I plan _____ back home tomorrow.

A. go   B. going   C. goes   D. to go

( ) 4. —It's a little cold today. Would you mind _____ the window?

—Of course not.

A. not opening   B. not to open   C. don't open   D. no opening

( ) 5. I prefer _____ to the library and museum on the weekends.

A. went   B. going   C. goes   D. go

( ) 6. I've got to make _____ he told a lie.

A. that clear   B. it clear that   C. quite clear   D. this clear that

( ) 7. My students begin _____ for the final examination recently.

A. prepare   B. preparing   C. to prepare   D. prepares

( ) 8. Last night we saw two movies, _____ was interesting.

A. both of which   B. neither of which

C. both of them   D. neither of them

( ) 9. — Jack seems like a good student. — He is always the first _____ his work.

A. finishes   B. finishing   C. finished   D. to finish

( ) 10. I often hear her _____ this song in the classroom after class.

A. sing   B. to sing   C. singing   D. sings

( ) 11. They are busy _____ the old car.

A. with mend   B. mend   C. to mend   D. mending

( ) 12. —Where are all the boys?

—I saw them _____ on the playground.

A. to play   B. played   C. plays   D. playing

( ) 13. I'm sorry _____ you that you didn't pass the math exam.

A. tell   B. told   C. to tell   D. telling

( ) 14. —Remember _____ him about it before he goes away.

—Sure, I will.

A. tell   B. to tell   C. telling   D. to telling

( ) 15. We must keep the classroom _____.

A. clean   B. to clean   C. cleaning   D. cleaned

( ) 16. The headmaster told us _____ at the Summer Palace on time.

　　　　A. arrive　　　B. arrived　　　C. arriving　　　D. to arrive

(　　) 17. You'd better _____ an umbrella with you. It is going to rain later on.

　　　　A. to take　　　B. taking　　　C. take　　　D. taken

(　　) 18. I told Jane _____ her homework before Friday.

　　　　A. finish　　　B. finishes　　　C. finishing　　　D. to finish

(　　) 19. Would you please _____ some water with you? It's so hot today, and you'll feel thirsty.

　　　　A. to take　　　B. take　　　C. not take　　　D. taking

(　　) 20. Please stop _____ a rest if you feel tired.

　　　　A. to have　　　B. having　　　C. have　　　D. has

(　　) 21. Although they are tired, they still go on _____.

　　　　A. working　　　B. to work　　　C. work　　　D. worked

(　　) 22. His grandparents don't work any more because they want _____ their life.

　　　　A. enjoy　　　B. enjoyed　　　C. enjoying　　　D. to enjoy

(　　) 23. Your son has kept _____ for two hours. You'd better ask him to have a rest.

　　　　A. study　　　B. studied　　　C. to study　　　D. studying

(　　) 24. —Do you know whether the man _____ by the door is Mr. Smith?

　　　　—Sure. We've known each other for a long time.

　　　　A. stand　　　B. standing　　　C. stood　　　D. stands

(　　) 25. It's dangerous _____ with the wild animals.

　　　　A. for us to play　　　　　　B. of us playing

　　　　C. for us playing　　　　　　D. of us to play

(　　) 26. —When are you going to have your hair _____?

　　　　—This afternoon.

　　　　A. cut　　　B. to cut　　　C. cutting　　　D. cuts

(　　) 27. Drivers shouldn't be allowed _____ after drinking, or they will break the law.

　　　　A. drive　　　B. driving　　　C. to drive　　　D. drives

(　　) 28. We don't know _____ it next. Let's go and ask Mr. Li.

　　　　A. what to do　　B. to do what　　C. whether to do　　D. to do whether

(　　) 29. Our English teacher encourages us _____ part in all kinds of after-class activities.

　　　　A. to take　　　B. take　　　C. taking　　　D. to taking

(　　) 30. How kind you are! You always do what you can _____ me.

　　　　A. help　　　B. helping　　　C. to help　　　D. helps

二、找出下列句子中错误的选项,并改正过来

1. There will have a film in my school tomorrow.
        A   B   C   D

2. Could you buy any apples for me?
     A   B   C   D

3. I will read English every morning, so my English is very good.
     A   B   C   D

4. There is a few orange in the glass. Would you like some?
        A   B   C   D

5. What about go to the seaside to swim?
     A B   C   D

6. Please be carefully. There is a dog near here.
    A   B   C   D

7. You are welcome in my home.
    A B   C   D

8. I'd like you go with me to the movie.
    A   B C   D

9. After a discussion, we decided order train tickets.
     A   B   C   D

10. My son likes flies kites more than anything else.
     A   B   C   D

1.(　)应为_____　　2.(　)应为_____　　3.(　)应为_____

4.(　)应为_____　　5.(　)应为_____　　6.(　)应为_____

7.(　)应为_____　　8.(　)应为_____　　9.(　)应为_____

10.(　)应为_____

For Better Performance

一、找出与所给单词画线部分读音相同的选项

(　) 1. mineral   A. driver   B. guide   C. library   D. winter

(　) 2. life   A. liter   B. biscuit   C. coastline   D. disaster

(　) 3. graduation   A. active   B. radio   C. radium   D. courage

(　) 4. beach   A. head   B. dead   C. breakfast   D. seaman

(　) 5. bench   A. stomach   B. watch   C. moustache   D. ache

Unit 1　Festivals Around the World

二、英汉互译

1. fall on ＿＿＿＿＿＿＿＿　　2. similar to ＿＿＿＿＿＿＿＿

3. receive your invitation ＿＿＿＿＿＿＿＿　　4. knock on ＿＿＿＿＿＿＿＿

5. trick or treat ＿＿＿＿＿＿＿＿　　6. ……的开始＿＿＿＿＿＿＿＿

7. 更喜欢做某事＿＿＿＿＿＿＿＿　　8. 圣诞老人＿＿＿＿＿＿＿＿

9. 冲走,洗掉＿＿＿＿＿＿＿＿　　10. ……的最后＿＿＿＿＿＿＿＿

三、用单词的适当形式填空

1. How about ＿＿＿＿＿＿（keep）an English diary every day?

2. You should practise ＿＿＿＿＿＿（speak）English as much as you can.

3. Don't forget ＿＿＿＿＿＿（do）some exercise when you are free.

4. Try ＿＿＿＿＿＿（not be）afraid of making mistakes when you speak English.

5. Tom ＿＿＿＿＿＿（forget）to do his homework yesterday.

6. How about ＿＿＿＿＿＿（go）swimming this weekend?

7. I am so happy ＿＿＿＿＿＿（receive）your invitation.

8. It is difficult for me ＿＿＿＿＿＿（remember）all the new words.

9. You can improve your spoken English by ＿＿＿＿＿＿（join）an English club.

10. Why don't you ＿＿＿＿＿＿（listen）to some music when you are tired?

四、找出下列句子中错误的选项,并改正过来

1. I would live in Nanjing when I was at primary school.
　　A　　　　　　　B　C　D

2. It falls to the first day of the first Chinese lunar month.
　　　　A　B　　　　　　　　　C　　　　D

3. Nobody knows the exact age of the earth by certain.
　　　　　A　　　　B　　C　　D

4. He raised his arm to protect his face to the blow.
　　　A　　　　B　　　　　　　C　D

5. I plan to go back home and celebrate a festival to my family.
　　　　A　　　　B　　　　　C　　　　　　D

1.(　　)应为＿＿＿＿　　2.(　　)应为＿＿＿＿　　3.(　　)应为＿＿＿＿

4.(　　)应为＿＿＿＿　　5.(　　)应为＿＿＿＿

单元检测

第一部分 英语知识运用(共分三节,满分40分)

第一节 语音知识:从 A、B、C、D 四个选项中找出其画线部分与所给单词画线部分读音相同的选项。(共5分,每小题1分)

( )1. exist　　A. exit　　　B. example　　C. expect　　D. excellent

( )2. peace　　A. breast　　B. theatre　　C. beach　　　D. ocean

( )3. shock　　A. polonium　B. devote　　　C. honor　　　D. discover

( )4. debt　　　A. habit　　　B. above　　　C. club　　　　D. climb

( )5. barbecue A. forward　　B. warm　　　C. popular　　D. kindergarten

第二节 词汇与语法知识:从 A、B、C、D 四个选项中选出可以填入空白处的最佳选项。(共25分,每小题1分)

( )6. —Can you give an example to show how useful a computer is?
　　—Sure. _____ people get _____ information from it every day.
　　A. A large number of; plenty of　　B. The number of; a lot of
　　C. Lots of; a lot　　　　　　　　　D. Many a; a great deal of

( )7. He is looking for another job because he feels that nothing he does _____ his boss.
　　A. serve　　　B. satisfies　　　C. promises　　　D. supports

( )8. Last Saturday Tom didn't wake up _____ the clock rang.
　　A. since　　　B. because　　　C. until　　　　　D. for

( )9. —Our new teacher's English is difficult for me to _____.
　　—Why don't you ask your brother _____ help?
　　A understand; with　　　B. follow; for
　　C. speak; for　　　　　　D. pick up; by

( )10. Nancy was writing a letter _____ mother came back.
　　A. after　　　B. before　　　C. if　　　　　　D. when

( )11. He dropped the _____ and broke it.
　　A. cup of coffee　　　　　B. coffee's cup
　　C. cup for coffee　　　　 D. coffee cup

( )12. —May I have _____ honor of dining with you?
　　—Sure, I feel quite honored, because you are _____ honor to our city.
　　A. an; the　　B. the; an　　C. the; the　　D. an; an

Unit 1　Festivals Around the World

(　　)13. I can't go with you together, _____ I'm busy doing my housework.
　　A. if　　　　B. because　　　C. until　　　　D. before

(　　)14. We are all looking forward _____ the Great Wall during the National Day.
　　A. to visiting　B. to visit　　C. for visiting　D. for a visit to

(　　)15. The great day he looked forward to _____ at last.
　　A. coming　　B. come　　　　C. came　　　　D. having come

(　　)16. It looks _____ you are ill. You should go to see the doctor.
　　A. as　　　　B. as though　　C. which　　　　D. whether

(　　)17. Our parents love us without expecting anything _____.
　　A. in turn　　B. in return　　C. for turn　　　D. for return

(　　)18. We were deeply _____ by the _____ movie *Wolf Warriors*.
　　A. moved; moved　　　　　B. moving; moved
　　C. moved; moving　　　　　D. moving; moving

(　　)19. She couldn't wait _____ after having online classes for such a long time.
　　A. to go to school　　　　　B. goes to school
　　C. going to school　　　　　D. was going to school

(　　)20. My younger brother _____ climbing the mountains at weekends.
　　A. keep in touch with　　　B. gets into the habit of
　　C. be in the habit of　　　　D. have the habit of

(　　)21. I felt _____ when I heard that he was _____ hurt.
　　A. terribly; terrible　　　　　B. terrible; terrible
　　C. terrible; terribly　　　　　D. terribly; terribly

(　　)22. Bill couldn't help _____ when he was watching the FIFA World Cup Qatar 2022.
　　A. laugh　　B. to laugh　　　C. laughing　　　D. laughs

(　　)23. Please tell me _____ you are feeling after getting Covid-19.
　　A. what　　　B. how　　　　C. when　　　　D. where

(　　)24. —I wish you success and have a good time in Beijing.
　　—_____.
　　A. The same to you　　　　B. That's OK
　　C. No problem　　　　　　D. Thank you

(　　)25. Making hand shadows made us all _____.
　　A. laughed　B. laughter　　　C. laughing　　　D. laugh

(　　)26. The young couple _____ every winter.
　　A. goes on a holiday　　　　B. were going on a holiday
　　C. go on a holiday　　　　　D. was going on a holiday

(　　)27. _____ happy family!
　　A. How　　　B. What　　　　C. What a　　　　D. How a

(   )28. Jenny _____ an hour in cleaning the classroom yesterday.
   A. took   B. cost   C. paid   D. spent

(   )29. I want to know if you are willing _____ me a hand?
   A. lend   B. to lend   C. lent   D. lending

(   )30. They plan to play _____ tennis after having _____ picnic next weekend.
   A. the; a   B. a; a   C. a; /   D. /; a

第三节　完形填空：阅读下面的短文，从所给的 **A、B、C、D** 四个选项中选出正确的答案。（共 10 分，每小题 1 分）

August the 15th, according to the lunar calendar（阴历）, is the traditional Mid-Autumn Festival in China. The festival is the second most important festival after the Spring Festival to Chinese people. Every year, when the __31__ comes, people go home from every corner of the world to __32__ their family and have dinner with them.

China's Mid-Autumn Festival is __33__ celebrated on the fifteenth day of the eighth lunar month.

Why is the Mid-Autumn Festival so __34__? It is related to the moon and Chinese people like the __35__ very much. In Chinese culture, the full moon is a symbol of peace and prosperity for the whole family. Its __36__ symbolizes wholeness and togetherness. In the middle of the eighth __37__ of the Chinese calendar the moon is full, and eight is also a/an __38__ number in Chinese culture, symbolizing prosperity and __39__. So people believe this day is very fortunate.

The Mid-Autumn Festival has a __40__ of 2000 years. During these 2000 years, lots of Mid-Autumn traditions have been thought up by Chinese people.

(   )31. A. festival B. holiday C. vocation D. celebration
(   )32. A. meet   B. visit   C. interview D. talk
(   )33. A. naturally B. certainly C. traditionally D. commonly
(   )34. A. various B. ordinary C. important D. traditional
(   )35. A. story   B. moon   C. moon cake D. culture
(   )36. A. roundness B. brightness C. length   D. bigness
(   )37. A. year   B. week   C. day   D. month
(   )38. A. right   B. exact   C. lucky   D. positive
(   )39. A. love   B. health   C. future   D. wealth
(   )40. A. civilization B. time   C. history   D. experience

第二部分　篇章与词汇理解（共分三节　满分 50 分）

第一节　阅读理解：阅读下列短文，从每题所给的 **A、B、C、D** 四个选项中，选出最恰当的答案。（共 30 分，每小题 2 分）

A

I have been in England three months now. I hope you don't think I've forgotten you.

There have been so many places to see and so many things to do that I've not had much time for writing letters.

I shall soon be starting my studies at King's College. So far I've been learning about England and British ways of living. I won't tell you about London. There are lots of books you can read and lots of pictures you can look at about this famous city. I'm sure you'll be more interested to know what I think about life here.

I find some of the customs interesting. People here do not shake hands as much as we do in the mainland(大陆) of Europe. During the first few weeks, I was often surprised because people did not put out their hands when I met them. Men raise their hats to women but not to each other.

(　　)41. The writer came to London from _____.

  A. Asia   B. the mainland of Europe

  C. America   D. Africa

(　　)42. The writer did not write the letter earlier because _____.

  A. she had forgotten her friend

  B. she was lonely and sad in this strange land

  C. she was too busy to write

  D. she was too busy with her courses(课) at King's College

(　　)43. How does the writer feel about British ways of living? _____.

  A. Happy   B. Angry   C. Sad   D. Interesting

(　　)44. The writer came to London _____.

  A. to make a living   B. to study

  C. to learn British ways of living   D. for sightseeing only

(　　)45. Englishmen _____.

  A. do not often shake hands with friends when they meet

  B. often shake hands when they meet with friends

  C. raise their hats to all friends when they meet

  D. do not raise their hats to any of their friends when they meet

B

A young father was visiting an old neighbor. They were standing in the old man's garden. and talking about children. The young man said,"How strict should parents be with their children?"

The old man pointed to a string between a big strong tree and a thin young one,"Please untie that string,"he said. The young man untied it, and the young tree bent over to one side. "Now tie it again, please,"said the old man," but first pull the string tight so that the young tree is straight again."

The young man did so, then the old man said, "There it is the same with children, You must be strict with them. but sometimes you must untie the string to know how they are getting on. If they are not yet able to stand alone, you must tie the string tight again. But when you find that they are ready to stand alone, you can take the string away."

( )46. The story is about _____.

A. how to take care of young trees

B. how to tie and untie the string

C. how the young father should get on with his old neighbor

D. how strict parents should be with their children

( )47. The young man untied the string _____.

A. in order to throw it away

B. so that both of the trees would grow straight

C. only to find that the thinner one bent over to one side

D. in order to let the old man teach him

( )48. When can the string be taken away? _____.

A. When the old man has left

B. After you have untied it

C. When the young man has untied it next time

D. When the young tree grows strong enough

( )49. At last the old man told the young man _____.

A. that he should be strict with his children if they could not yet stand alone

B. that he should always be strict with his children

C. that he should be hard on them

D. that he should tie his children until they are ready to stand alone

( )50. In the story, the relation(关系) of the big strong tree to the thin one is like that of _____.

A. the young father to the old neighbor

B. grown-ups to their parents

C. the old neighbor to the children of the young father

D. parents to their children

C

People in the United States honor their parents with 2 special days: Mother's Day on the second Sunday in May and Father's Day on the 3rd Sunday in June. These days are to show love and respect for parents. They raise their children and educate them to be responsible citizens. They give love and care. These two days offer an opportunity to think about the changing roles of mothers and fathers. More mothers now work outside the home and more fathers must help with childcare.

These two special days are celebrated in many different ways. On mother's Day, people wear carnations. A red one symbolizes a living mother. A white one shows that the mother is dead. Many people attend religious services to honor parents. It's also a day when people whose parents are dead visit the cemetery(grave). On these days, families get together at home as well as in

Unit 1　Festivals Around the World

restaurants. They often have outdoor barbecue for Father's Day. These are days of fun and good feelings and memories.

　　Another tradition is to give cards and gifts. Children make them in school. Many people make their own presents. These are more valued than those bought in stores. It's not the value of the gift that is important, but "the thought that counts". Greeting card stores, florists, candy makers, bakers, phone companies and other stores do lots of business during these holidays.

(　　)51. Which is NOT a reason for children to show love and respect for parents? _____

　　A. Parents bring up children.

　　B. Parents give love and care to children.

　　C. Parents educate children to be good persons.

　　D. Parents pass away before children grow up.

(　　)52. What do you know from the passage? _____

　　A. Both festivals are in May.

　　B. Fewer women worked outside the home in the past.

　　C. Not all the children respect their parents.

　　D. Fathers are not as important as mothers at home.

(　　)53. Which do you know about "carnation"? _____

　　A. It only has two kinds of color.

　　B. It refers to the special clothes people wear on Mother's Day.

　　C. It's a kind of flower showing love and best wishes.

　　D. People can wear them only on the second Sunday in May.

(　　)54. On Mother's Day and Father's Day _____.

　　A. people sometimes have family parties

　　B. everyone goes to the cemetery

　　C. children always go to parents' home

　　D. hand-made cards are the most valuable gifts

(　　)55. What do you think "florists" do? _____

　　A. They sell flowers.

　　B. They make bread or pastry.

　　C. They offer enough room for having family parties.

　　D. They sell special clothes for Mother's Day and Father's Day.

第二节　词义搭配：从(B)栏中选出(A)栏单词的正确解释。(共10分，每小题1分)

　　　　　　A　　　　　　　　　　　　　　B

(　　)56. respect　　　　A. full of high spirits and fun

(　　)57. symbol　　　　B. a feeling of admiration

(　　)58. craft　　　　　C. something represents a more general quality

( )59. harvest   D. full of light
( )60. appreciate   E. to show that a day or an event is important
( )61. bright   F. to show or make known a feeling
( )62. celebrate   G. showing something
( )63. express   H. the act of cutting
( )64. playful   I. an activity involving a special skill at making
( )65. sign   J. to recognize the good qualities of sth

第三节 补全对话：根据对话内容，从对话后的选项中选出能填入空白处的最佳选项。(共10分，每小题2分)

Lisa：Hi,Mary！Merry Christmas！

Mary： 66 Hey, I've heard you got a prize in the English speech contest.

Lisa： 67

Mary：Congratulations！It's really hard work to prepare for an English speech contest.

Lisa：Yeah, and sometimes I even wanted to give up.

Mary： 68

Lisa：I'd like to thank you for your help.

Mary： 69

Lisa：Right！How would you like to celebrate？

Mary： 70

Lisa：Great！Let's go.

A. Have dinner first and then go to KTV.
B. But now you are successful in the contest.
C. Merry Christmas！
D. How about a celebration？
E. Yeah,I got the second place.

第三部分 语言技能运用(共分四节 满分30分)

第一节 单词拼写：根据下列句子及所给汉语注释，在横线上写出该单词。(共5分，每小题1分)

71. People splash water at each other in a _____ (嬉戏的) manner.

72. The typical tradition is eating _____ (月饼).

73. People splash water at one another as a _____ (标志) of happiness and good luck for the coming year.

74. It's a _____ (团聚) time for families and friends.

75. People prefer going to the temple fairs to buy traditional _____ (工艺品).

Unit 1　Festivals Around the World

第二节　词形变换：用括号内单词的适当形式填空,将正确答案写在横线上。(共 5 分,每小题 1 分)

76. The government decide _____ (rebuild) the Center Street.

77. I was _____ (annoy) that they had not turned up.

78. This restaurant has a _____ (cheer) atmosphere.

79. Most of the _____ (interview) said that they wanted to do things in their own ways.

80. I have my _____ (free) and like you, I have my own opinions.

第三节　改错：从 A、B、C、D 四个画线处找出一处错误的选项,并写出正确答案。(共 10 分,每小题 2 分)

81. <u>Following</u> the <u>road</u> and you will <u>find</u> the <u>store</u>.
　　　A　　　　　B　　　　　　C　　　D

82. Its tail, <u>which</u> is white, <u>moving</u> up and <u>down</u> as it <u>runs</u>.
　　　　　　A　　　　　　B　　　　　C　　　　D

83. I was often <u>tired</u> and <u>watch</u> TV <u>demands</u> little <u>effort</u>.
　　　　　　　A　　　B　　　　C　　　　D

84. It was kind of <u>them</u> to <u>meet</u> me at the station and <u>drove</u> me to <u>their</u> home.
　　　　　　　A　　　B　　　　　　　　C　　　　　D

85. Please excuse us <u>for</u> <u>not</u> <u>able</u> to say goodbye <u>to</u> you.
　　　　　　　　A　B　　C　　　　　　　D

81. ( )应为 _____　　82. ( )应为 _____　　83. ( )应为 _____
84. ( )应为 _____　　85. ( )应为 _____

第四节　书面表达(共 10 分)

作文题目：A traditional Chinese festival。

词数要求：80~100 词。

写作要点：介绍一个中国的传统节日。(可以介绍其历史来源、民间故事,等等)

Unit 2

Community Life

Warming-up

一、句型汇总

1. Could you tell me the way to the nearest supermarket? 您能告诉我去最近的超市的路吗?

2. What other facilities do we have? 我们还有什么其他的设施?

3. Is there a place where I can exercise? 这里有我可以运动的地方吗?

4. By the way, is there a beauty salon in the community? 顺便问一下,小区里有美容院吗?

5. Do you want to live closer to a cinema? 您想住得离电影院更近一些吗?

6. It is very important to find the right school for the kids. 对于孩子们来说找到合适的学校非常重要。

7. You should get a real feel for the neighborhood. 你应该好好感受一下这个社区。

8. Why not go to the hair salon, which is just behind the laundry? 为什么不去发廊呢? 它就在洗衣店后面。

9. The house, which you like best, will be sold tomorrow. 你最喜欢的房子明天就会被卖掉的。

10. This is the neighborhood that they visited last summer holiday. 这就是他们去年暑假参观过的那个社区。

Unit 2　Community Life

11. Water is a must for everyone to live. 水是每个人的必需资源。

12. Please share your location with me, then, I will know where you are. 请您共享您的位置给我,然后我就能知道您在哪里。

二、英汉互译

1. convenience store ＿＿＿＿＿＿＿＿

2. community ＿＿＿＿＿＿＿＿

3. 设施＿＿＿＿＿＿＿＿

4. neighborhood ＿＿＿＿＿＿＿＿

5. 目的 ＿＿＿＿＿＿＿＿

6. opposite ＿＿＿＿＿＿＿＿

7. medicine ＿＿＿＿＿＿＿＿

8. transportation ＿＿＿＿＿＿＿＿

9. 干洗店＿＿＿＿＿＿＿＿

10. environment ＿＿＿＿＿＿＿＿

11. 电影院＿＿＿＿＿＿＿＿

12. 位置＿＿＿＿＿＿＿＿

13. important ＿＿＿＿＿＿＿＿

14. 适合 ＿＿＿＿＿＿＿＿

Listening and Speaking

一、找出与所给单词画线部分读音相同的选项

(　　)1. l<u>o</u>cal　　A. mel<u>o</u>n　　B. fl<u>o</u>wer　　C. s<u>ea</u>son　　D. gr<u>o</u>w

(　　)2. m<u>u</u>st　　A. <u>au</u>tumn　　B. <u>u</u>pset　　C. <u>u</u>sually　　D. t<u>ou</u>r

(　　)3. f<u>a</u>cility　　A. tr<u>ai</u>n　　B. v<u>a</u>cation　　C. m<u>a</u>tter　　D. pr<u>a</u>ctice

(　　)4. l<u>i</u>festyle　　A. l<u>i</u>st　　B. po<u>i</u>nt　　C. pr<u>i</u>ze　　D. <u>i</u>nformation

(　　)5. d<u>i</u>strict　　A. c<u>e</u>nter　　B. l<u>o</u>cation　　C. f<u>e</u>nce　　D. c<u>e</u>lebrate

二、从 B 栏中找出与 A 栏中相对应的答语

A

1. Could you tell me the way to the convenience store?
2. Is there a beauty salon in the community?
3. What other facilities do we have?
4. Why is this community is suitable for Mr. Brown?
5. Do you want to live closer to a cinema?

B

> A. Yes, because I like watching movies.
> B. Oh, we don't have one yet.
> C. Turn right at the end of this path and you will see it.
> D. We also have hair salon, laundry and a clinic in this community.
> E. Because there is a school near here.

三、用所给句子补全下面对话

A: Excuse me, Madame? Could you tell me the way to the nearest supermarket?

B: 1   But why not shop in the convenience store in our community?

A: Convenience store?   2

B: It's just behind Building 8, near the main gate. Are you new here?

A: Yes, I just moved in two days ago. By the way,   3

B: Oh, there is a restaurant for the elderly. And there is a very nice garden just in the center of our community.

A: That's good.   4

B: Yes, there is a fitness center which is open from 9:00 am to 12:00 pm every day.

A: Great. And is there a clinic?

B: 5

A: It's really convenient to live in this community. Thank you very much.

B: You are welcome.

> A. By the way, is there a place where I can exercise?
> B. Yes, It's on Xinhua Road, about 15 minutes' walk from here.
> C. No, we don't have one yet, but there's a hospital opposite our community.
> D. Where is it?
> E. What other facilities do we have?

四、场景模拟

假如你想买一所房子，去售楼处询问有关小区内部设施的一些情况，为情境编写一个对话。

提示词汇：facilities/clinic/school/beauty salon/by the way

Reading and Writing

一、用单词的适当形式填空

1. Could you tell me the way to the _____ (near) clinic?
2. It's about 5 _____ (分钟) walk from here.
3. Do you want _____ (居住) closer to a cinema?
4. It is very important _____ (find) the right school for the kids.
5. Nothing is _____ (important) than taking a walk to get a real feel for the neighborhood.
6. People like to visit certain websites _____ (分享) their living experiences.
7. I enjoy _____ (watch) movies that can encourage young people.
8. Please share your location with me, then I _____ (知道) where you are.
9. The community is _____ (locate) in a district where there are several school.
10. The countryside is _____ (attract) more and more visitors from the city on weekends.

二、完形填空

I'm now living in a small house with my parents. Our life is __1__ but happy. I must study hard so I can buy a big new __2__ some day. I call it my __3__ house. My dream house has three floors __4__ five bedrooms, three bathrooms, two big dining rooms and two living rooms. When my friends come to visit me, I will have enough __5__ for them to live in. We'll have a good time together. Besides that, we will have a __6__ behind the house. When summer comes, my friends and I can swim in it. We will also have a garden in front of the house. In the morning, my parents can do some exercise in the __7__. We can also grow some flowers and __8__ in it. The flowers will be beautiful, and the vegetables will be nice to eat. When we feel tired, we can have a good rest in it. Life will be easy and __9__ for us. I like my dream house very much. My friends also think it's __10__. I'll study hard, so my dream can come true.

( )1. A. easy   B. hard   C. comfortable   D. nice
( )2. A. room   B. classroom   C. house   D. balcony
( )3. A. dream   B. big   C. small   D. beautiful
( )4. A. and   B. have   C. has   D. with
( )5. A. food   B. drinks   C. bedrooms   D. fruit
( )6. A. swimming pool   B. garden   C. balcony   D. Kitchen

( )7. A. park B. garden C. sitting room D. bedroom
( )8. A. vegetables B. green trees C. fruit trees D. small animals
( )9. A. unhappy B. tired C. comfortable D. difficult
( )10. A. sad B. wonderful C. hard D. uncomfortable

三、阅读理解

阅读下面短文，从每题所给的 A、B、C、D 四个选项中选出最佳答案。

I live in a city, since I was small, our family moved to the neighborhood. I have lived in the neighborhood for about ten years. I spend my childhood here, I make many friends, I get to know all the children here. I am so happy to live in the neighborhood. People here just like a big family. In the morning, the old like to dance and walk in the neighborhood, while the young do some jogging. In the afternoon, kids play together after school. At night, most people go out in the square after dinner. They share the things happened on that day, people laugh happily. The neighborhood is a big home for me. I know everyone here, it is a paradise.

( )1. How many years does the writer lived in the neighborhood?
   A. Five. B. Ten. C. Eight. D. We don't know.

( )2. Does the writer have friends in the neighborhood?
   A. Yes, he does. B. No, he doesn't.
   C. No, he does. D. Sorry.

( )3. What do the old like to do in the morning?
   A. Dance. B. Walk.
   C. Dance and walk. D. Do some jogging.

( )4. What do the kids like to do after school?
   A. Laugh. B. Dance.
   C. Share the things. D. Play together.

( )5. The neighborhood is a _____ for me.
   A. house B. paradise C. school D. garden

四、书面表达

你理想中的小区是什么样的？请用英语描述出来吧。

提示词汇：neighborhood/garden/dance/be full of/clean

Grammar

一、从下面每小题四个选项中选出最佳选项

( ) 1. Is this the factory _____ you visited last week?
　　A. that　　　B. where　　　C. in which　　　D. the one

( ) 2. The wolves hid themselves in the places _____ couldn't be found.
　　A. that　　　B. where　　　C. in which　　　D. in that

( ) 3. I'll tell you _____ he told me last week.
　　A. all which　B. that　　　C. all that　　　D. which

( ) 4. I have bought the same skirt _____ she is wearing.
　　A. as　　　　B. that　　　C. which　　　　D. what

( ) 5. He failed in the examination, _____ made his mother very angry.
　　A. which　　B. it　　　　C. that　　　　　D. what

( ) 6. We're talking about the piano and the pianist _____ were in the concert we attended last weekend.
　　A. which　　B. whom　　C. who　　　　　D. that

( ) 7. The boy _____ an English song in the next room is Lily's brother.
　　A. who is singing　B. is singing　　C. sang　　　D. was singing

( ) 8. Those _____ not only from books but also through practice will succeed.
　　A. learn　　B. who　　　C. that learns　　D. who learn

( ) 9. Anyone _____ this opinion may speak out.
　　A. that against　B. that is against　C. who is against　D. who are against

( ) 10. Didn't you see the woman _____?
　　A. I nodded just now
　　B. whom I nodded just now
　　C. I nodded to her just now
　　D. I nodded to just now

( ) 11. Can you lend me the book _____ the other day?
　　A. that you talked
　　B. you talked about it
　　C. which you talked with
　　D. you talked about

( ) 12. Is there anything _____ to you?
　　A. that is belonged
　　B. that belongs
　　C. that belong
　　D. which belongs

(   ) 13. —"How do you like the novel?"

　　　　—"It's quite different from _____ I read last month."

　　　　A. that　　　B. which　　　C. the one　　　D. the one what

(   ) 14. Mr. Li gave the textbooks to all the pupils except _____ who had already taken them.

　　　　A. the ones　　　B. ones　　　C. some　　　D. the others

(   ) 15. The train _____ he was travelling was late.

　　　　A. which　　　B. where　　　C. on which　　　D. in that

(   ) 16. He has lost the key to the drawer _____ the gifts are kept.

　　　　A. where　　　B. in which　　　C. under which　　　D. which

(   ) 17. Antarctic _____ we know very little is covered with thick ice all the year round.

　　　　A. which　　　B. where　　　C. that　　　D. about which

(   ) 18. It's the second time _____ late this week.

　　　　A. that you arrived　　　　B. when you arrived

　　　　C. that you've arrived　　　D. when you've arrived

(   ) 19. It was in 1969 _____ the American astronaut succeeded in landing on the moon.

　　　　A. that　　　B. which　　　C. when　　　D. in which

(   ) 20. May the fourth is the day _____ we Chinese people will never forget.

　　　　A. which　　　B. when　　　C. on which　　　D. about which

(   ) 21. We are going to spend the Spring Festival in Hangzhou, _____ live my grandparents and some relatives.

　　　　A. which　　　B. that　　　C. who　　　D. where

(   ) 22. The hotel _____ during our holidays stands by the seaside.

　　　　A. we stayed at　　　　B. where we stayed at

　　　　C. we stayed　　　　　D. in that we stayed

(   ) 23. Is it in that factory _____ "Red Flag" cars are produced?

　　　　A. in which　　　B. where　　　C. which　　　D. that

(   ) 24. He is not _____ a fool _____.

　　　　A. such, as he is looked　　　B. such, as he looks

　　　　C. as, as he is looked　　　　D. so, as he looks

(   ) 25. He has two sons, _____ work as chemists.

　　　　A. two of whom　　　B. both of whom

C. both of which   D. all of whom

(   )26. I, _____ your good friend, will try my best to help you out.
     A. who is   B. who am   C. that is   D. what is

(   )27. I can't understand _____.
     A. what does Christmas mean   B. what Christmas does mean
     C. what mean Christmas does   D. what Christmas means

(   )28. Could you tell me _____ the radio without any help?
     A. how did he mend   B. what did he mend
     C. how he mended   D. what he mended

(   )29. There is only one thing _____ I can do.
     A. what   B. that   C. all   D. which

(   )30. Houses _____ locations are in the best school districts will hold their value better and are attractive to value buyers.
     A. that   B. who   C. where   D. whose

二、找出下列句子中错误的选项，并改正过来

1. This <u>is</u> Qin Shi Huang, who <u>was</u> the <u>one</u> emperor in <u>China</u>.
     A   B   C   D

2. Don't <u>get</u> too <u>close</u> to the house <u>who</u> roof is under <u>repair</u>.
           A   B   C   D

3. Here's how <u>to find</u> a neighborhood <u>where</u> is just right <u>for</u> <u>you</u>.
            A   B   C D

4. Now, the <u>first</u> local <u>intelligent</u> community has <u>built</u> at Ganjiakou Community <u>in</u> Beijing.
        A   B   C   D

5. There <u>is</u> a café <u>in</u> the community, <u>which</u> he can <u>enjoy</u> his spare time.
        A   B   C   D

6. I <u>am</u> sure you will <u>find</u> one <u>you</u> like <u>it</u>.
   A   B   C   D

7. She has to <u>work</u> if she <u>wants</u> to <u>live</u> <u>comfortable</u>.
          A   B   C   D

8. One day I <u>wrote</u> a little <u>story</u> and <u>showed</u> to <u>my</u> teacher.
         A   B   C   D

9. There were <u>too</u> many nice <u>things</u> that I <u>didn't</u> know <u>what</u> to choose.
          A   B   C   D

10. He decides to <u>travel</u> a lot and <u>visit</u> <u>such</u> many new <u>places</u> as possible.
            A   B C   D

1.(   )应为_____   2.(   )应为_____   3.(   )应为_____
4.(   )应为_____   5.(   )应为_____   6.(   )应为_____
7.(   )应为_____   8.(   )应为_____   9.(   )应为_____

10.（　　）应为_____

For Better Performance

一、找出与所给单词画线部分读音相同的选项

(　　) 1. l<u>au</u>ndry   A. l<u>au</u>gh   B. <u>au</u>nt   C. bec<u>au</u>se   D. <u>au</u>tumn

(　　) 2. l<u>i</u>st   A. cl<u>i</u>mb   B. l<u>i</u>tter   C. l<u>i</u>ght   D. l<u>i</u>ke

(　　) 3. neighborh<u>oo</u>d   A. bl<u>oo</u>d   B. w<u>oo</u>d   C. f<u>oo</u>l   D. sch<u>oo</u>l

(　　) 4. p<u>ur</u>pose   A. t<u>ur</u>n   B. Sat<u>ur</u>day   C. s<u>ur</u>prise   D. after

(　　) 5. s<u>u</u>it   A. <u>u</u>nless   B. <u>u</u>niversity   C. <u>u</u>pset   D. tr<u>u</u>st

二、英汉互译

1. get a feel for _____
2. opposite to _____
3. shopping mall _____
4. instead of _____
5. beauty salon _____
6. have a chance _____
7. fitness center _____
8. 便利店 _____
9. 检验 _____
10. 满足某人的需求 _____

三、用所给词的适当形式填空

1. Is there a place where I can _____ (buy) some medicine?

2. Why not _____ (shop) at the convenience store in our community?

3. I _____ (move) into a new community two days ago.

4. Everything you want about local schools can _____ (find) on our homepage.

5. I think Community A is _____ (suit) for Mr. Zhang.

6. There is a swimming pool, which can _____ (perfect) meet his needs.

7. Then you will have a good chance _____ (find) a neighborhood that suits your lifestyle.

8. I hate _____ (阅读) books that are only full of boring jokes.

9. A swimming pool is a must for me, because I'm used to _____ (游泳) everyday.

10. This is a kind of cup, which ancient _____ (中国) drank wine with.

四、找出下列句子中错误的选项,并改正过来

1. The water <u>in</u> this community <u>is</u> so dirty that it <u>smells</u> <u>terribly</u>.
             A   B   C   D

2. I visited <u>a</u> place <u>where</u> <u>is</u> surrounded by <u>mountains</u>.
             A   B   C   D

3. They didn't want <u>me</u> <u>to do</u> any <u>work</u> at <u>family</u>.
                    A   B   C   D

4. Henry did not <u>like</u> his car, <u>that</u> ran <u>badly</u> and often <u>broke</u> down.
                A   B   C   D

5. He had <u>lost</u> his <u>glasses</u> without <u>them</u> he couldn't <u>see</u>.
        A   B   C   D

1.(　　)应为_____　2.(　　)应为_____　3.(　　)应为_____

4.(　　)应为_____　5.(　　)应为_____

单元检测

第一部分　英语知识运用(共分三节,满分40分)

第一节　语音知识:从 A、B、C、D 四个选项中找出其画线部分与所给单词画线部分读音相同的选项。(共5分,每小题1分)

(　　)1. gr<u>a</u>de　　A. w<u>a</u>lk　　B. loc<u>a</u>tion　　C. neckl<u>a</u>ce　　D. <u>a</u>round

(　　)2. s<u>ou</u>th　　A. c<u>ou</u>rage　　B. s<u>ou</u>p　　C. s<u>ou</u>thern　　D. tr<u>ou</u>sers

(　　)3. smoo<u>th</u>　　A. fea<u>th</u>er　　B. too<u>th</u>　　C. <u>th</u>ief　　D. warm<u>th</u>

(　　)4. offi<u>c</u>ial　　A. <u>c</u>oncert　　B. <u>c</u>entury　　C. <u>c</u>oast　　D. o<u>c</u>ean

(　　)5. <u>li</u>festyle　　A. faci<u>li</u>ty　　B. <u>li</u>st　　C. <u>li</u>vely　　D. important

第二节　词汇与语法知识:从 A、B、C、D 四个选项中选出可以填入空白处的最佳选项。(共25分,每小题1分)

(　　)6. Zhang Dong loves writers _____ write their own stories.

    A. which　　B. who　　C. has worked　　D. whose

(　　)7. I like music _____ I can dance to.

    A. whom　　B. when　　C. who　　D. that

(　　)8. We Chat is an invention _____ can help people talk to friends, share photos, ideas and feelings freely.

    A. which　　B. who　　C. what　　D. whom

(   )9. The research he had devoted himself _____ a perfect success.

  A. to proved   B. proved   C. to prove   D. to proving

(   )10. —What did you do last night, Tom?

  — I viewed the video _____ was recorded in the Tiangong space station.

  A. who   B. what   C. which   D. whom

(   )11. —Do you know the boy _____ is sitting next to Peter?

  —Yes. He is Peter's friend. They are celebrating his _____ birthday.

  A. who; ninth   B. that; nineth   C. /; nineth   D. which; ninth

(   )12. —What kind of movies do you like?

  —I like movies _____ are about Chinese history.

  A. who   B. whom   C. whose   D. that

(   )13. The supermarket is only 15 _____ walk away from here.

  A. minute   B. minutes   C. minute's   D. minutes'

(   )14. Children _____ don't like exercising will put on weight easily.

  A. who   B. which   C. what   D. how

(   )15. There will be a stamp show in the museum _____ we visited last week.

  A. who   B. when   C. which   D. what

(   )16. The speech contest, _____ is "Man and Nature", will be held in Room 10 from 2:00 to 5:00 _____ the afternoon of May the tenth.

  A. which topic; on   B. whose topic; on

  C. that topic; in   D. the topic of that; in

(   )17. She heard a terrible noise, _____ brought her heart into her mouth.

  A. it   B. which   C. this   D. that

(   )18. —What are you doing?

  —I am reading a book by Mo Yan _____ you lent me last week.

  A. whether   B. what   C. who   D. which

(   )19. —Our English teacher is very kind, and we all like her very much.

  —That's for sure. A person _____ cares for others is popular everywhere.

  A. who   B. which   C. whom   D. whose

(   )20. It's impossible for anyone to take the sovereignty(主权) over Taiwan Island away from China, _____ has been part of China since ancient times.

  A. where   B. that   C. which   D. it

(   )21. Of all the countries, China is _____ one in fighting COVID-19.

  A. successful   B. more successful   C. most successful   D. the most successful

Unit 2　Community Life

(　　) 22. —Who is _____ student to get to school in your class?

　　—Tom, he is always he first one to go to school.

　　　A. the early　　B. the earliest　　C. the last　　D. the latest

(　　) 23. Today I can see a hall full of talented teens graduated from Changsha Vocational School, _____ eyes are full of hope for the future.

　　　A. where　　B. who　　C. whose　　D. that

(　　) 24. Mr. Zhong Nanshan, _____ helped the Chinese overcome SARS in 2003, also plays a very important role in the fight against COVID-19.

　　　A. that　　B. which　　C. who　　D. what

(　　) 25. Can you tell me the way _____ the nearest clinic?

　　　A. by　　B. to　　C. of　　D. in

(　　) 26. _____ is very important to keep healthy in daily life.

　　　A. That　　B. It　　C. What　　D. That

(　　) 27. The house, which you like best, will _____ tomorrow.

　　　A. sell　　B. sold　　C. be sold　　D. selling

(　　) 28. Please share your location _____ me, then, I will know where you are.

　　　A. to　　B. with　　C. from　　D. about

(　　) 29. The countryside is attracting more and more _____ from the city on weekends.

　　　A. visit　　B. visitors　　C. visitor　　D. visits

(　　) 30. Is there a place _____ I can take a walk?

　　　A. who　　B. when　　C. which　　D. where

第三节　完形填空：阅读下面的短文，从所给的 A、B、C、D 四个选项中选出正确的答案。(共 10 分，每小题 1 分)

　　When my children were young, I used to read to them every evening before bed. One of their favorite stories was called, *Somebody Loves You, Mr. Hatch*. Mr. Hatch lived a __31__ life. He walked alone to work every day and ate his lunch alone in a corner. He never smiled. He never talked to __32__ on his way home. In the evening he would read a newspaper and go to bed early.

　　His life changed, however, on Valentine's Day when he got a heart-shaped box full of chocolate in the mail, along with a note that said, "Somebody loves you." At first, he couldn't believe it, but as he let the message sink in, he began to laugh and dance around. That single message had opened his heart to the __33__ of love. Soon he found himself being __34__. He became a joy at work and began to __35__ people in the neighborhood. As the days and weeks went by, his laughter, smiles, kindness, happiness and love __36__ everyone in his community.

　　Later, Mr. Hatch found out that the heart-shaped box had been delivered to him __37__. He

— 29 —

felt upset and went back to his old ways. When his neighbors found out, however, they decided not to lose the light he shared. They surprised him with a __38__ and a huge banner(条幅) that read,"Everybody Loves Mr. Hatch. " Mr. Hatch cried when he realized that somebody loved him __39__.

I think that we all have a tiny bit of Mr. Hatch in us. At times we all feel unloved and unlovable. __40__, somebody does love us. May the pages of your life story be full of love.

( )31. A. happy   B. rich   C. hard   D. lonely

( )32. A. someone   B. everyone   C. anyone   D. no one

( )33. A. meaning   B. power   C. result   D. nature

( )34. A. respectful   B. peaceful   C. successful   D. cheerful

( )35. A. stare at   B. learn from   C. help out   D. compete with

( )36. A. touched   B. supported   C. saved   D. persuaded

( )37. A. on purpose   B. in return   C. by mistake   D. in secret

( )38. A. party   B. letter   C. newspaper   D. competition

( )39. A. at times   B. after all   C. with pleasure   D. in public

( )40. A. Instead   B. However   C. Besides   D. Therefore

第二部分　篇章与词汇理解(共分三节　满分50分)

第一节　阅读理解:阅读下列短文,从每题所给的A、B、C、D四个选项中,选出最恰当的答案。(共30分,每小题2分)

A

When you have a dinner party, what should you do? The following will help you. Try to open the door for each guest. If someone else answers the door, go to welcome your guests as soon as you can. Always offer(主动) to take their coats and ask,"Would you like me to take your coat?"

People often bring gifts(礼物) like flowers or chocolate to a dinner party. Be ready to receive(收到) the gifts if they do. Get a vase so that you can put the flowers in it. Never leave a guest unattended(没人照顾的), especially when there is only one of them. If there is more than one, they can talk to each other.

If the party is at home, a good idea is to have a toilet(洗手间) sign(指示牌) for people who don't know your house.

If the party is somewhere else, like a restaurant, try not to be too loud, because not everyone in the restaurant is at your party.

( )41. The text tells us _____.

　　　　　A. how to choose a gift　　　　B. how to be a polite guest

　　　　　C. how to make friends at a party　D. how to have a dinner party

(　　)42. When your guests arrive, you should take their _____ for them.

　　　　　A. coats　　　B. gifts　　　C. shoes　　　D. flowers

(　　)43. If you go to a dinner party, you can take _____ as a gift according to the text.

　　　　　A. clothes　　B. vegetables　C. chocolates　D. fruit

(　　)44. What does the underlined word "vase" mean in Chinese?

　　　　　A. 水壶　　　B. 花瓶　　　C. 礼盒　　　D. 保温瓶

(　　)45. Which of the following is NOT true according to the text?

　　　　　A. It is not good to leave a guest unattended.

　　　　　B. You must open the door for every guest.

　　　　　C. It is better to have a toilet sign.

　　　　　D. People can have dinner parties at home or in a restaurant.

B

　　Imagine you are living in a moving house. Inside the house, there is a small kitchen, bathroom and bedroom.

　　Everything you need is close at hand.

　　In the US, you can really see these moving houses on the mad. They are called recreational vehicles(RV, 房车). People call them houses on wheels. When it's holiday time, the whole family often gets into this lovely house and hits the road for a trip across the country.

　　Compared to a real house, this home on the road is small for a family who has to spend every hour of every day together. But the best thing about it is that it changes your journey into a free exploration.

　　You can drive as long as you like without worrying about finding hotels. Or you can just stop somewhere nice and stay for a few weeks. You may also come across other families who are on road trips. Together, you take out your tents and snacks. It's camping time with a lot of chat and laughter.

　　Of course, RVs are not always convenient(便利). They can sometimes break down and you have to spend time mending them. But this type of road trip still wins people's hearts because they can go whenever and wherever they want.

(　　)46. _____ RVs, everything you need is close at hand.

　　　　　A. Inside　　B. Outside　　C. Behind　　D. Beside

(　　)47. In the US, people call RVs moving _____.

　　　　　A. cars　　　B. wheels　　C. houses　　D. buses

( )48. Which of the following about RVs is TRUE? _____
   A. They don't have any wheels
   B. They are always convenient.
   C. They are bigger than real houses
   D. They may break down sometimes.

( )49. Why do people prefer traveling in RVs? _____
   A. They like eating snacks in RVs.
   B. They can explore their journey freely.
   C. They may leave RVs in hotels for a few weeks.
   D. They will never come across other traveling families.

( )50. What's the best title of the passage? _____
   A. A Road Trip   B. A Wonderful House
   C. Moving Homes to Travel   D. Holiday Life in the US.

C

When it comes to shopping for clothes, my mother and I have always disagreed on what fits me well. To me, if it zips, it fits. My mom, however, usually tells me I need a bigger size.

When I was a teenager, I wanted to dress like my friends, but my body size made it impossible. When mom told me something didn't suit me, or I needed a bigger size, all I heard was that my body was wrong.

To avoid arguments, we stopped going shopping together. This continued until I got engaged (订婚) last year and needed to buy some clothes. When I tried on a blouse, my mother looked at me, and I knew what was coming. "You need a bigger size," she said.

There was no bigger size. I tried to hold back my tears(眼泪). Maybe I could buy it alone, of course, but my mom is my favorite person to hang out with. The idea of looking for a wedding dress without her seemed just as scary as taking her with me.

And so the day came. As I tried on a simple white dress, I saw tears in my mom's eyes. "You look beautiful!" She told me. Nothing could have shocked me more.

This one didn't zip up at the back and I did actually need a bigger size, but my mother didn't say that. She just told me how beautiful I looked. In that moment, all the arguments in the past ended. We didn't buy a dress that day. We decided to see more.

A few weeks later, we found the perfect dress. We both loved it as soon as I put it on.

And during those few weeks, mom and I also found the perfect fit for our shopping relationship.

( )51. What does the writer want to show in the first two paragraphs?
   A. She likes the clothes with zippers while her mother doesn't agree with her.

B. In mom's opinion, her body is wrong and she is too fat to wear what she likes.

C. She really wants to dress like her friends, but her mom doesn't allow her to do so.

D. She and mom always disagree on what clothes fit her because of wrong understanding.

(　　)52. How did the writer probably feel after she tried on the simple white dress?

A. Funny and surprised.　　B. Shocked and sorry.

C. Proud and moved.　　D. Excited and scary.

(　　)53. What does the underlined sentence in Paragraph 4 mainly mean?

A. I couldn't shop for a wedding dress myself because my mom disagreed.

B. I felt kind of scary when I went shopping with my mother for a wedding dress.

C. I felt like shopping for a wedding dress with mom though she thought it was scary.

D. I wanted to shop for a wedding dress alone but I couldn't stand shopping without mom.

(　　)54. Which is the best word to describe the perfect fit for their shopping relationship?

A. Missing.　　B. Embarrassing.　　C. Understanding.　　D. Encouraging.

(　　)55. What's the main idea of the text?

A. Praising makes the perfect fit for their shopping relationship.

B. Tears sure the best way to end arguments between family members.

C. Love is everything in good communication between family members.

D. Better communication requires not only love but also a more suitable way.

第二节　词义搭配：从（B）栏中选出（A）栏单词的正确解释。（共10分，每小题1分）

A	B
(　　)56. attractive	A. The way we live
(　　)57. compare	B. a place or business where clothes, etc. are washed and ironed
(　　)58. district	C. a building or place that provides a particular service or is used for a particular industry
(　　)59. gym	D. athletic facility equipped for sports or physical training
(　　)60. facility	E. an area of a country or town, especially one that has particular features
(　　)61. laundry	F. consider or describe as similar, equal, or analogous
(　　)62. lifestyle	G. A place
(　　)63. location	H. the people who lived each other
(　　)64. purpose	I. A goal or meaning in your life

( )65. neighborhood　　J. having power to arouse interest

第三节　补全对话：根据对话内容，从对话后的选项中选出能填入空白处的最佳选项。(共10分，每小题2分)

A：Hello, is that Miss White?

B：Yes, it is. __66__

A：I'm from the package delivery company(快递公司). Here's your package. Are you at home?

B：Unluckily, I'm at work right now. __67__

A：In fact, I need to give it to you in person. Can I bring it to your workplace, instead?

B：__68__ I don't even have time to get it.

A：I see. __69__

B：Yes, that would be better. Can you bring it to my home at 5：00 p.m. tomorrow?

A：Sure, I can do that. __70__

B：See you, thanks.

> A. I'm quite busy working now.
> B. What can I do for you?
> C. Well, can I bring the package tomorrow?
> D. See you tomorrow.
> E. Can you leave the package at my door?

第三部分　语言技能运用(共分四节　满分30分)

第一节　单词拼写：根据下列句子及所给汉语注释，在横线上写出该单词。(共5分，每小题1分)

71. The _____ (设施)in our school is very complete and convenient.

72. I often play badminton in the _____ (体育馆).

73. We have to have the washing done at the _____ (洗衣店).

74. It was a big change in _____ (生活方式)when you moved to the country.

75. My _____ (目的) is going to a good university in a few months.

第二节　词形变换：用括号内单词的适当形式填空，将正确答案写在横线上。(共5分，每小题1分)

76. If you want to have good _____ (tooth), you need to brush them every day.

77. She always _____ (take) a walk after dinner.

78. My mother thinks _____ (get) up too late isn't good for my health.

79. Scott has an _____ (interest) job at radio station.

80. Please brush your teeth at least _____ (two) a day.

第三节 改错：从 A、B、C、D 四个画线处找出一处错误的选项，并写出正确答案。(共 10 分，每小题 2 分)

81. Is there a place <u>that</u> I can <u>buy</u> some <u>medicine</u>?
      A   B C   D

82. <u>Children</u> should <u>allowed</u> to spend time <u>playing</u> with <u>their</u> friends.
  A   B   C   D

83. We must pay <u>attention</u> to the <u>pronounce</u> <u>when</u> we read <u>words</u>.
       A   B   C   D

84. <u>My</u> sister often <u>studies</u> by <u>make</u> flash <u>cards</u>.
  A   B   C   D

85. Can you <u>told</u> the <u>different</u> <u>between</u> the two <u>pictures</u>?
     A   B   C   D

81. (　　) 应为 _____　　82. (　　) 应为 _____　　83. (　　) 应为 _____
84. (　　) 应为 _____　　85. (　　) 应为 _____

第四节 书面表达(共 10 分)

作文题目：My community。

词数要求：80~100 词。

写作要点：介绍一下你所在的社区。(提示：有什么建筑物和设施、是否方便，做简单的解释说明)

_____

_____

_____

_____

_____

Unit 3

Artificial Intelligence

Warming-up

一、句型汇总

1. I don't think so. 我不这样认为。

2. I agree with you！我同意你的观点。

3. All the dishes cooked by robots are as delicious as those made by chefs. 机器人做的所有的菜和厨师做的一样美味。

4. It is humans that design and control robots. 是人类制造和控制了机器人。

5. AI helps lower costs and improve efficiencys. 人工智能降低了成本，提高了效率。

6. In terms of costs and efficiency, we are on the same page. 在成本和效率方面，我们是一致的。

7. There was no one working on the assembly line. 没有人在装配线上工作。

8. To be honest, I prefer traditional restaurants. 说句实话，我更喜欢传统的餐馆。

9. AI is used in many fields. 人工智能在许多领域被应用。

10. Many people hold a welcoming attitude towards AI. 许多人对人工智能持欢迎的态度。

11. The increasing use of AI does bring some obvious benefits. 人工智能的使用确实明显地给大家带来了一些好处。

12. We have more time to enjoy our life. 我们有更多的时间来享受生活。

13. Our work is serving the people. 我们的工作就是为人民服务。

14. AI causes risks or even disasters if not used properly. 如果没有正确使用，人工智能会引起风险甚至灾难。

15. AI frees people from heavy labor. 人工智能把人们从繁重的劳动中解脱出来。

二、英汉互译

1. 交流 _____   2. 灾难 _____
3. 教育 _____   4. 提高 _____
5. 明显的 _____   6. 恰当的 _____
7. advantage _____   8. attitude _____
9. benefit _____   10. risk _____
11. efficiency _____   12. serve _____

Listening and Speaking

一、找出与所给单词画线部分读音相同的选项

(   ) 1. appl<u>y</u>   A. att<u>i</u>tude   B. appl<u>i</u>cation   C. l<u>o</u>cation   D. anoth<u>e</u>r
(   ) 2. r<u>i</u>sk   A. b<u>i</u>ke   B. l<u>i</u>st   C. l<u>i</u>festyle   D. fe<u>s</u>tival
(   ) 3. b<u>e</u>nefit   A. <u>e</u>njoyable   B. <u>i</u>mprove   C. ch<u>e</u>ck   D. r<u>e</u>ceive
(   ) 4. disa<u>s</u>ter A. prope<u>r</u>ly   B. <u>s</u>erve   C. <u>t</u>erm   D. he<u>r</u>
(   ) 5. <u>s</u>erve   A. di<u>s</u>aster   B. <u>o</u>bvious   C. <u>c</u>ause   D. bag<u>s</u>

二、从 B 栏中找出与 A 栏中相对应的答语

A   B

1. AI can bring benefits to human being.   A. No problem!
2. Is mobile payment very convenient?   B. I agree with you.
3. I think AI will be positive for human.   C. It can be used in assembly line.
4. Can you help me with the heavy box?   D. I don't think so.
5. Where can AI be used?   E. Yes, it is.

三、用所给句子补全下面对话

A: Good morning, __1__ ?

B: Good morning, I want to buy a sweeping robot.

A: How about this one? __2__

B: It looks nice. __3__ ?

A: Yes, you can press this button to operate it.

B: It sounds good. I will take it.

A: __4__

B: I will pay by phone.

A: OK, __5__ .

> A. please scan the QR code to pay.
> B. It is the latest product of our store.
> C. Are you paying it in cash or by card?
> D. What can I do for you?
> E. Is it easy to operate?

四、场景模拟

就人工智能和你朋友编写一组对话，谈论你对人工智能的看法。

提示词汇：worry about/take place of in many fields/free… from/I think…

Reading and Writing

一、用单词的适当形式填空

1. The invention would have wide _____ （应用）in industry.

2. The new thing will _____ （受益）both sides.

3. AI helps lower cost and improve _____ （效率）.

4. It is really amazing, there is no one working in the _____ （生产）line.

5. His height gives him a clear _____ （优势）.

6. The new discovery may be _____ （apply）in medicine.

7. The _____ （cause）of the fire is not yet known.

8. Losing your job doesn't have to be such a _____ （disaster）.

9. She came up with a new idea for _____ （increase）sales.

10. He was very _____ （obviously）in his distrust of us.

二、完形填空

"Robot teachers, who never get angry or speak unpleasant words, have been popular among pupils in some Korean school," A reporter said.

School __1__ were glad to answer robot teachers' questions in class. Scientists sent English-teaching robots to three schools for eight __2__ teaching in December, 2009. And last November, robot teachers teaching math, science __3__ art came to five schools in Seoul, the capital of Korean.

Scientists __4__ that the English-teaching robots helped raise interest in the __5__ and the confidence of students.

Scientists say that sending robot teachers to school is __6__ to rural school children. They can lean __7__ in this way. School children are __8__ in studying when robot teachers __9__ lessons to them. They can also make students more __10__. Scientists are now trying to make robot teachers better quality. What will the students be if their teachers are all robot teachers? Let's wait and see.

( ) 1. A. boys   B. girls   C. teachers   D. students
( ) 2. A. week's   B. weeks'   C. week   D. weeks
( ) 3. A. and   B. but   C. or   D. if
( ) 4. A. thought   B. knew   C. found   D. wanted
( ) 5. A. art   B. PE   C. music   D. language
( ) 6. A. helpful   B. careful   C. thankful   D. beautiful
( ) 7. A. a lot of   B. lots of   C. lot of   D. a lot
( ) 8. A. interest   B. interested   C. surprise   D. surprised
( ) 9. A. have   B. give   C. take   D. send
( ) 10. A. outgoing   B. beautiful   C. creative   D. careful

三、阅读理解

阅读下面短文,从每题所给的 A、B、C、D 四个选项中选出最佳答案。

From self-driving cars to carerobots (看护机器人) for elderly people, rapid development in technology has long represented a possible threat to many jobs normally performed by people. But experts now believe that almost 50 percent of occupations existing today will be completely unnecessary by 2025 as artificial intelligence (人工智能) continues to change businesses.

"The next fifteen years will see a revolution (革命) in how we work, and a revolution will necessarily take place in how we plan and think about workplaces," said Peter Andrew, director of Workplace Strategy for CBRE Asia Pacific. A growing number of jobs in the future will require creative intelligence, social skills and the ability to use artificial intelligence.

The report is based on interviews with 200 experts, business leaders and young people from Asia Pacific, Europe and North America. It shows that in the US technology already destroys more jobs than it creates. But the report states: "Losing occupations does not necessarily mean losing jobs — just changing what people do." Growth in new jobs could occur as much, according to the research. "The growth of 20 to 40 person companies that have the speed and technological knowledge will directly challenge big companies," it states.

A 2014 report by Pew Research Centre found 52 percent of experts in artificial intelligence and robotics were optimistic about the future and believed there would still be enough jobs in the next few years. "The optimists pictured a future in which robots do not take the place of more jobs than they create," according to Aaron Smith, the report's co-author.

"Technology will continue to affect jobs, but more jobs seem likely to be created. Although there have always been unemployed people, when we reached a few billion people there were billions of jobs. There is no shortage of things that need to be done and that will not change," Microsoft's Jonathan Grudin told researchers.

( )1. We can infer from the text that in the future _____.

  A. people will face many difficulties

  B. people will take up more creative jobs

  C. artificial intelligence will threaten people's lives

  D. most jobs will be done in traditional workplaces

( )2. According to the report, _____.

  A. small companies will win against big companies

  B. big companies will face fewer challenges

  C. people won't necessarily lose jobs

  D. most people will become interested in technology

( )3. What is the attitude of most experts in artificial intelligence and robotics to the future? _____.

  A. Mixed   B. Hopeful   C. Worried   D. Doubtful

( )4. Jonathan Grudin's words in the last paragraph suggest that _____.

  A. there will be enough jobs for people

  B. things will change a lot in a few years

  C. many people will become unemployed

  D. technology will totally change future jobs

(　　)5. What will a growing number of jobs in the future require? _____.

　　A. Creative intelligence

　　B. Social skills

　　C. The ability to use artificial intelligence

　　D. All the above

四、书面表达

以 AI and our life 为题,写一篇作文,谈谈 AI 在日常生活中的应用。字数 80~100 字。

_____
_____
_____
_____
_____

Grammar

一、从下面每小题四个选项中选出最佳选项

(　　)1. I live in a house _____ a beautiful garden in front of it.
　　A. is having　　B. have　　C. having　　D. had

(　　)2. The person _____ with Mike is her brother.
　　A. talk　　B. to talk　　C. talking　　D. talked

(　　)3. Mary has a dress _____ of cotton.
　　A. make　　B. to make　　C. making　　D. made

(　　)4. Do you know the man _____ at the school gate?
　　A. stand　　B. is standing　　C. stood　　D. standing

(　　)5. The story _____ by Lu Xun is popular in China.
　　A. is writing　　B. written　　C. to write　　D. writes

(　　)6. The next thing he saw smoke _____ from behind the house.
　　A. rose　　B. rising　　C. to rise　　D. risen

(　　)7. Look over there, there's a very long, winding path _____ up to the house.
　　A. leading　　B. leads　　C. led　　D. to lead

(　　)8. Recently a survey _____ prices of the same goods in two different store caused heated debate among citizens.

  A. compared B. comparing C. compares D. being compared

(　　) 9. Tsinghua University _____ in 1911, is home to a great number of outstanding figures.

  A. found B. founding C. founded D. to be found

(　　) 10. The ability _____ an idea is as important as the idea itself.

  A. expressing B. expressed C. to express D. to be expressed

(　　) 11. The players _____ from the whole country are expected to bring us honor in this summer game.

  A. selecting B. to select C. selected D. having selected

(　　) 12. The island _____ to the mainland by a bridge, is easy to go to.

  A. joining B. to join C. joined D. having joined

(　　) 13. The rare fish _____ from the cooking pot, has been returned to the sea.

  A. saved B. saving C. to be saved D. having saved

(　　) 14. Mrs. White showed her students some old maps _____ from the library.

  A. to borrow B. to be borrowed C. borrowed D. borrowing

(　　) 15. I have a lot of readings _____ before the end of this term.

  A. completing B. to complete C. completed D. being completed

(　　) 16. I'm calling to enquire about the position _____ in yesterday's *China Daily*.

  A. advertised B. to be advertised C. advertising D. having advertised

(　　) 17. The traffic rule says young children under the age of four and _____ less than 40 pounds must be in a child safety seat.

  A. being weighed B. to weigh

  C. weighed D. weighing

(　　) 18. His first book _____ next month is based on a true story.

  A. published B. to be published C. to publish D. being published

(　　) 19. So far nobody has claimed the money _____ in the library.

  A. discovered B. to be discovered C. discovering D. discovers

(　　) 20. We are invited to a party _____ in our club next Friday.

  A. to be beld B. held C. being held D. holding

(　　) 21. For breakfast he only drinks juice from fresh fruit _____ on his own farm.

  A. grown B. being grown C. to be grown D. to grow

(　　) 22. A new book _____ by a young student is becoming popular now.

  A. write B. to write C. written D. writing

(   )23. The play _____ next month aims mainly to reflect the local culture.
　　　A. produced　　B. being produced　C. to be produced　D. having been produce

(   )24. With the world changing fast, we have something new _____ with all by ourselves every day.
　　　A. deal　　　B. dealt　　　C. to deal　　　D. dealing

(   )25. With the government's aid, those _____ by the earthquake have moved to the new settlements.
　　　A. affect　　B. affecting　　C. affected　　D. were affected

(   )26. You should make yourself _____ pretty well if you keep on speaking the language.
　　　A. understood　B. understand　C. to understand　D. understanding

(   )27. It is one of the funniest things _____ on the Internet so far this year.
　　　A. finding　　B. being found　　C. to find　　D. found

(   )28. —Can those _____ at the back of the classroom hear me?
　　　—No problem.
　　　A. seat　　　B. sit　　　C. seated　　　D. sat

(   )29. The trees _____ in the storm have been moved off the road.
　　　A. being blown down　　　　B. blown down
　　　C. blowing down　　　　　　D. to blow down

(   )30. At the beginning of class, the noise _____ the desks could be heard outside the classroom.
　　　A. opened and closed　　　　B. to be opened and closed
　　　C. opening and closing　　　　D. open and close

二、找出下列句子中错误的选项，并改正过来

1. In China, policemen are brave enough save people's lives.
　　A　　　　B　　　　　　　　　C　　D

2. Smart phones making by Huawei are getting more and more popular.
　　　　　　　A　　　　B　　　　　　C　　　　　D

3. Do you know the girl talked with Mr. Wang over there.
　A　　　　　　　　B　　C　　　　　D

4. A new song to write by a young singer is becoming very popular now.
　　　　　A　B C　　　　D

5. My friend Mike wants to join the swim club, and he swims well.
　　　　　　　　A　　B　　　C　　　　　　　　　D

6. You need people working to the benefit of the community.
　　　　　　A　　B　　　　　C　　　　D

7. AI works in same way as people.
      A   B   C   D

8. We can see robot worked in the store.
     A   B   C D

9. The stealing wallet was found by the policeman.
      A   B   D

10. She thought out a good idea for increase sales.
       A   B   C   D

1.(　　)应为_____　　2.(　　)应为_____　　3.(　　)应为_____

4.(　　)应为_____　　5.(　　)应为_____　　6.(　　)应为_____

7.(　　)应为_____　　8.(　　)应为_____　　9.(　　)应为_____

10.(　　)应为_____

For Better Performance

一、找出与所给单词画线部分读音相同的选项

(　　)1. pr<u>a</u>ctice　　A. <u>e</u>njoyable　　B. f<u>a</u>cility　　C. <u>a</u>ppreciate　　D. sn<u>a</u>ck

(　　)2. <u>o</u>bvious　　A. sym<u>bo</u>l　　B. l<u>o</u>cal　　C. c<u>o</u>mpare　　D. b<u>o</u>x

(　　)3. <u>e</u>ffect　　A. g<u>e</u>t　　B. <u>e</u>njoyable　　C. r<u>e</u>union　　D. b<u>e</u>e

(　　)4. ques<u>tion</u>　　A. applica<u>tion</u>　　B. educa<u>tion</u>　　C. sugges<u>tion</u>　　D. ac<u>tion</u>

(　　)5. <u>c</u>elebrate　　A. <u>c</u>ause　　B. s<u>c</u>an　　C. <u>c</u>lock　　D. ra<u>c</u>e

二、英汉互译

1. 说句实话 _____　　2. 导致 _____

3. 同意某人 _____　　4. 多亏 _____

5. 意见一致 _____　　6. 依靠 _____

7. QR code _____　　8. pros and cons _____

9. credit card _____　　10. thanks for _____

11. have effect on _____　　12. mobile payment _____

三、用单词的适当形式填空

1. We must study hard so that we can _____ (serve) the people better in the future.

2. I think _____ (AI) has a good promise on the web.

3. Now most people use _____ (mobile) payment instead of paying in cash.

— 44 —

4. It is said that all the dishes was _____（cook）by robots.

5. Our life is getting more _____（enjoy）and convenient.

6. _____（教育）is one of the most important things in a country.

7. I need to _____（提高）my English writing ability.

8. Mary asks me how to _____（应用）the computer.

9. Mike can _____（交流）with people freely in Chinese.

10. Whether we will go _____（依赖）on the weather.

四、找出下列句子中错误的选项，并改正过来

1. Be sure that you and the other students are in the same page.
　　　A　　　　B　　　　　　　　　　C　D

2. Thank you to your help with my English.
　　　　　A　　B　　C　　D

3. Answer the phone while driving may lead to death.
　　A　　　　　　B　　C　　　　D

4. The Smiths arrived Beijing and visited the Great Wall.
　　　　A　　B　　　　C　　D

5. He finished her homework without making any mistakes.
　　　　　　A　　　　　　B　　　C　　D

1.（　）应为_____　2.（　）应为_____　3.（　）应为_____

4.（　）应为_____　5.（　）应为_____

单元检测

第一部分　英语知识运用（共分三节，满分40分）

第一节　语音知识：从 A、B、C、D 四个选项中找出其画线部分与所给单词画线部分读音相同的选项。（共5分，每小题1分）

（　）1. aunt　　A. because　　B. cause　　C. autumn　　D. laugh

（　）2. attitude　A. communication　B. lunar　　C. cup　　D. blue

（　）3. depend　A. efficiency　　B. appreciate　C. reunion　D. temple

（　）4. practice　A. gala　　B. snack　　C. water　　D. craft

（　）5. husband　A. spring　　B. harvest　　C. must　　D. disaster

第二节　词汇与语法知识： 从 A、B、C、D 四个选项中选出可以填入空白处的最佳选项。（共 25 分，每小题 1 分）

(　　) 6. I agree _____ him in many things, but not everything.
　　　A. to　　　　B. in　　　　C. with　　　　D. for

(　　) 7. After a short break, they went on _____ the song.
　　　A. to learn　　B. learning　　C. learns　　D. learned

(　　) 8. Tom often practices _____ English in the morning.
　　　A. speaking　　B. to speak　　C. speaks　　D. spoken

(　　) 9. Mary enjoys _____ football on Sundays.
　　　A. play　　　B. to play　　　C. playing　　D. played

(　　) 10. We were deeply _____ by the _____ movie *Wolf Warriors*.
　　　A. moved; moved　　　　B. moving; moved
　　　C. moved; moving　　　　D. moving; moving

(　　) 11. Melbourne is a beautiful city with huge garden, great parks and many _____ building.
　　　A. amazing　　B. amaze　　C. amazed　　D. to amaze

(　　) 12. It's _____ to talk about the future world.
　　　A. interested　　B. interesting　　C. to interest　　D. interest

(　　) 13. The best time _____ China is autumn.
　　　A. coming　　B. coming to　　C. come to　　D. to come to

(　　) 14. How much time do you spend _____ piano each time.
　　　A. practicing playing the　　　B. to practicing playing
　　　C. to practice to play the　　　D. practice to play

(　　) 15. We can communicate _____ people in every part of the world _____ the Internet.
　　　A. with, with　　　　B. with, through
　　　C. through, through　　D. through, with

(　　) 16. _____ the bad weather, the match had been cancelled.
　　　A. Thanks for　　B. Thanking for　　C. Thanking to　　D. Thanks to

(　　) 17. When you decided to _____ a job, the first thing _____ is to prepare a good resume.
　　　A. apply for, to do　　　　B. apply for, doing
　　　C. application, to do　　　D. application, doing

(　　) 18. A resume is a summary of your personal _____ and work _____.

A. education, experience   B. education, experiences
C. educations, experiences   D. educations, experience

(   )19. Smoke from _____ coal is one of the _____ of air pollution.
A. burning, effect   B. burning, causes
C. burnt, causes   D. burnt, effects

(   )20. In given conditions, a bad thing sometimes _____ good results.
A. lead to   B. leading to   C. leads to   D is led to

(   )21. The _____ speed of the new machine is much higher than that of the old one.
A. turn   B. turning   C. turns   D. turned

(   )22. I don't know the date for _____ the library.
A. open   B. opens   C. opening   D. to open

(   )23. Is there anybody _____ the work?
A. carry on   B. to carry on   C. carrying on   D. carried on

(   )24. Do you mind my brothers and sisters _____ with us?
A. coming   B. to come   C. came   D. comes

(   )25. He is looking for a room _____ in.
A. live   B. living   C. to live   D. lived

(   )26. He rides his bike _____ a car to work every day.
A. instead to drive   B. instead of drive
C. instead driving   D. instead of driving

(   )27. Advantage has been _____ of the child to steal a necklace from the store.
A. made   B. done   C. taken   D. used

(   )28. I'm glad _____ a visit to him last week.
A. to pay   B. paying   C. to have paid   D. having paid

(   )29. He desired nothing but _____ home.
A. go   B. to go   C. going   D. went

(   )30. _____ with the size of the whole earth, the biggest ocean doesn't seem big at all.
A. Compare   B. When compare   C. Comparing   D. When compared

第三节 完形填空：阅读下面的短文，从所给的 **A、B、C、D** 四个选项中选出正确的答案。(共10分,每小题1分)

With the __31__ of science and technology, AI is __32__ the way we live. And there is a hot discussion about whether __33__ a robot.

__34__ speaking, the advantages of having a robot can be listed __35__ follows. __36__ AI robot can work by following orders of human beings. In addition, an AI robot can __37__ in many fields, like transportation, medical treatment, smart home and other fields. __38__, there __39__ also some disadvantages. An AI robot is easy __40__ viruses and its battery life is not long.

( )31. A. develop   B. development   C. developing   D. to develop
( )32. A. changing   B. changed   C. to change   D. changes
( )33. A. buy   B. bought   C. to buy   D. buying
( )34. A. General   B. Generals   C. Generalist   D. Generally
( )35. A. as   B. to   C. of   D. in
( )36. A. The   B. /   C. An   D. a
( )37. A. be used   B. used   C. using   D. to use
( )38. A. and   B. so   C. or   D. However
( )39. A. is   B. are   C. be   D. was
( )40. A. infect   B. to infect   C. infects   D. infecting

第二部分   篇章与词汇理解(共分三节   满分50分)

第一节   阅读理解：阅读下列短文，从每题所给的A、B、C、D四个选项中，选出最恰当的答案。(共30分，每小题2分)

A

Wives of Belt and Road Forum("一带一路"国际论坛) leaders visited the Palace Museum with the wife of Chinese President Xi Jinping on May 15h, 2017. They came to China with their husbands for the great meeting. They hope to know more about China.

Peng Liyuan took them to visit the world's famous place—the Palace Museum. It is in the capital (首都) of China. On Monday, the visitors took photos in front of Taihe Dian at the Palace Museum. They listened to the old history of the Palace Museum and visit a show about some old special things. The visitors came to know old trade routes(贸易路线) from them.

Later Peng Liyuan took them to a garden of the Palace Museum. There was a show place about Beijing's programs. The visitors enjoyed some famous Chinese performances. They were interested in Chinese culture.

Peng Liyuan talked about her wish. She hoped that the visitors would play important roles in the friendly and helpful group between China and their home countries.

Belt and Road Forum began on May 14, 2017 and it was over on May 15. About 130 different country leaders joined the meeting in Beijing. Many countries know China and regarded(把……看作) China as their friend, and we hope to make it much better. We want to make every country stronger and stronger through Belt and Road.

(   )41. Wives of Belt and Road Forum leaders visited _____.

  A. the Palace Museum   B. the Great Wall

  C. zoo   D. summer palace

(   )42. The visitors did the following things in the Palace Museum except _____

  A. take photos.   B. make special things.

  C. watch famous performances.   D. listen to the old history.

(   )43. What does the underlined word "it" refer to? _____

  A. Beijing.

  B. The old trade route.

  C. The Belt and Road Forum.

  D. Friendship between China and other countries.

(   )44. What can't we know from the passage?

  A. The leaders of different countries also visited some other cities in China.

  B. How many countries joined the Bell and Road Forum.

  C. When the Belt and Road Forum ended.

  D. The wives of Belt and Road Forum leaders wanted to know more about China.

(   )45. Why did China hold (举办) "Belt and Road Forum"?

  A. China needed to know more country leaders.

  B. China needed help from other countries.

  C. China wanted to make every country stronger.

  D. China wanted to show the Palace Museum.

B

  Apple's logo is one of the most familiar icons(图标) around the world. But what's the story about the Apple logo? The image of the apple is obvious, because that's the name of the company. What about the bite? The famous story is that the logo shows respect and honor for Alan Turing. He was the father of computer science. He researched artificial intelligence(人工智能) and unlocked German wartime codes(密码). However, after the war, he was put into prison, because of his beliefs. He could not stand the looking down and chose to bite a poisoned apple to end his life in the prison.

  However, Rob Janoff, who designed the famous Apple logo, said, "It's not the truth, but only a legend. The real reason why I designed it with a bite is very simple. I wanted people to get that it was an apple not a cherry. When I go to markets to buy apples, I always mistake apples for cherries. It really has nothing to do with the scientist."

  Are you kidding? An apple is much bigger than a cherry. It's very easy to tell. But if you use an apple to design a logo, some people may mistake it for a cherry.

(   )46. Apple's logo is one of the most familiar _____ around the world.
  A. fruit   B. icons   C. food   D. picture

(   )47. The image of the apple is obvious, because that's the name of the _____.
  A. the designer B. tree C. company D. phone

(   )48. Both the apple and the cherry are almost the same in _____.
  A. weight   B. size   C. color   D. shape

(   )49. According to the passage, Alan Turing _____.
  A. used an apple to design a logo
  B. died in the prison
  C. was put into prison during the war
  D. was the father of a computer company

(   )50. What's the purpose of writing the passage about the apple logo?
  A. To introduce its designer. B. To tell us a legend about it.
  C. To try to find the truth of it. D. To explain its market research.

C

  The computer is fast, and never makes a mistake, while people are too slow and full of mistakes sometimes. That's what people often say when they talk about computers. For over a quarter of a century, scientists have been making better and better computers. Now a computer can do a lot of daily jobs wonderfully. It is widely used in factories, hospitals, post offices and airports. A computer can report, decide and control in almost every field. Many computer scientists are thinking of making the computer "think" like a man. With the help of a person, a computer can draw pictures, write music, talk with people, play chess, recognize voices, translate languages and so on. Perhaps computers will one day really think and feel. Do you think the people will be afraid when they find that the computer is too clever to listen to and serve the people? No, people will make better use of the computers in the future. Man is always the master of the computer. The computer works only with the help of man. It cannot take the place of man.

(   )51. According to the passage, we know that _____.
  A. at work, the computer is more effective than people
  B. the computer is widely used in many fields
  C. engineers have been working on the computers for more than twenty-five years
  D. A、B and C

(   )52. With the help of a person, a computer can do the following things except

_____.

A. fight with another computer B. draw pictures

C. translate languages D. write music

(　　)53. Computers are _____ the people.

A. going to control B. doing more and more jobs for

C. taking the place of D. making use of

(　　)54. Many computer scientists are now planning _____.

A. to make the computers too clever to listen to and serve the people

B. to make the computers take the place of people

C. to make the computer "think" like a man

D. to make the computers do many daily jobs

(　　)55. People will _____ the computers in the future

A. make better use of B. really be afraid of

C. no longer use D. help

第二节　词义搭配：从(B)栏中选出(A)栏单词的正确解释。(共10分,每小题1分)

A   B

(　　)56. improve   A. to make a formal request

(　　)57. apply   B. make or become better

(　　)58. perform   C. to offer, provide or give

(　　)59. supply   D. act or play

(　　)60. depend   E. raise, upgrade

(　　)61. lead to   F. manner to /towards

(　　)62. benefit   G. suitable, fittest

(　　)63. proper   H. result in, cause

(　　)64. disaster   I. rely on

(　　)65. attitude   J. suffering

第三节　补全对话：根据对话内容,从对话后的选项中选出能填入空白处的最佳选项。(共10分,每小题2分)

A：Hey, Bob. Today I have visited a car factory.

B：__66__

A：Yes, I saw the robots putting different parts of a car together. __67__

B：__68__.

A：Yes. It brings huge convenience and avoid some accidents.

B: __69__. I have seen a robot waiter working in the department store.

A: __70__. Our life is getting more enjoyable and convenient.

B: I agree with you.

> A. There is no one working on the assembly line.
> B. I think so.
> C. Now AI is used in many fields.
> D. Oh, it's amazing.
> E. Are there any interesting things?

第三部分　语言技能运用(共分四节　满分30分)

第一节　单词拼写：根据下列句子及所给汉语注释,在横线上写出该单词。(共5分,每小题1分)

71. You could _____ (申请) to be a nurse.

72. Here are some _____ (优势) we have in the match.

73. He got a lot of chances to _____ (表演) in movies.

74. We should _____ (依靠) ourselves in everything.

75. People who stole didn't _____ (受益) from ill-gotten gains.

第二节　词形变换：用括号内单词的适当形式填空,将正确答案写在横线上。(共5分,每小题1分)

76. The greenhouse _____ (effect) is well and truly with us.

77. We expected to see further _____ (improve) over the coming year.

78. Make sure the letter is properly _____ (address).

79. The guide _____ (lead) us to visit the palace yesterday.

80. Most people hold a _____ (welcome) attitude towards AI.

第三节　改错：从A、B、C、D四个画线处找出一处错误的选项,并写出正确答案。(共10分,每小题2分)

81. She <u>is</u> always <u>the</u> first <u>to come</u> and the last <u>leaving</u>.
　　　A　　　　B　　　　C　　　　　　　　D

82. He was <u>interesting</u> in <u>history</u> <u>when</u> he <u>was</u> a child.
　　　　　A　　　　　　B　　　C　　　　D

83. Can you get <u>me</u> <u>something</u> <u>eat</u>.
　　　　　　　A　　　B　　　　　C

84. The girl <u>sing</u> <u>in</u> the <u>next room</u> is his friend?
　　　　　　A　　B　　　　　　　D

85. It is <u>amazed</u> <u>that</u> the robot is <u>used</u> <u>in</u> the store.
　　　　　A　　B　　　　　　　C　D

81. (　)应为 _____　82. (　)应为 _____　83. (　)应为 _____
84. (　)应为 _____　85. (　)应为 _____

第四节　书面表达(共10分)

作文题目：随着人工智能的普及，人们对其有很大的争议。谈谈你对人工智能在日常生活中应用的担忧。

词数要求：80~100词。

Unit 4

Customer Service

Warming-up

一、句型汇总

1. There is something wrong with the mobile phone battery. 手机电池坏了。

2. We are very sorry for any in convenience caused. 我们对由此带来的不便深感抱歉。

3. I'd like to have the mobile phone repaired. 我想维修我的手机。

4. Since we have been partners for so long, we'll try our best to work out a better solution for you. 既然我们已经成为合作伙伴这么久了,我们将尽力为您找到更好的解决方案。

5. Even if I charge it for a whole night, it still does not work. 即使我充了一晚上电,它还是不能用。

6. Even though you didn't express such a request, we will reduce the price of the leaflets by 15%. 即使你没有提出这样的要求,我们也将降低传单价格的 15%。

7. Can I see your receipt so that I can check whether it is still under guarantee? 请出示您的收据,以便我们检查是否在保修期内。

8. Since it is our fault, we will pay for all your loss. 既然是我们的错误,我们会赔偿您一切损失。

9. He is so excited that he can hardly sleep. 他兴奋得几乎睡不着。

10. I am writing to complain about the delayed delivery of my order. 我写信投诉我的订单延迟交付。

11. We hope you can give us some discounts for future orders. 我们希望以后的订单可以给我们一些折扣。

12. Make sure the goods arrive on time. 确保货物按时到达。

13. There is something wrong with the mobile phone battery. 手机电池坏了。

14. Why don't you start early so that you don't have to hurry? 为什么你不早点出发,那样你就没必要着急了?

15. I think we should pay for the loss because it's our carelessness that caused the problem. 我认为我们应该弥补这个损失,因为是我们的粗心才导致。

二、英汉互译

1. 抱怨 _____   2. 收据 _____

3. 延迟 _____   4. 递送 _____

5. 不便 _____   6. 许诺 _____

7. in charge of _____   8. have…repaired _____

9. make a complaint _____   10. deal with _____

11. due to _____   12. make sure _____

Listening and Speaking

一、找出与所给单词画线部分读音相同的选项

(   ) 1. ap<u>o</u>logy   A. b<u>a</u>ttery   B. bl<u>a</u>nk   C. d<u>a</u>mage   D. adv<u>a</u>ntage

(   ) 2. <u>ch</u>eck   A. ex<u>ch</u>ange   B. <u>ch</u>emistry   C. stoma<u>ch</u>   D. <u>Ch</u>ristmas

(   ) 3. c<u>o</u>mplaint   A. pr<u>o</u>mise   B. l<u>o</u>cal   C. <u>o</u>bvious   D. c<u>o</u>mmunicate

(   ) 4. dama<u>g</u>e   A. <u>g</u>ym   B. <u>g</u>ive   C. <u>g</u>ain   D. <u>g</u>lad

(   ) 5. d<u>e</u>liver   A. b<u>e</u>d   B. b<u>e</u>nefit   C. d<u>e</u>lay   D. f<u>e</u>stival

二、从 B 栏中找出与 A 栏中相对应的答语

A

1. See you next time.
2. What's the problem?
3. I'm calling to complain about the wrong sizefor my shoes.
4. Would you please show me your receipt?
5. I will exchange a new one for you, is that OK?

B

A. Thank you!
B. We are sorry for any inconvenience caused by us.
C. There is something wrong with my bike.
D. See you.
E. Ok, here you are.

三、用所给句子补全下面对话

A：Excuse me, the shoes that I bought yesterday seem to have a problem.

B：___1___

A：You give me the wrong size.

B：___2___ Would you please show me your receipt?

A：___3___

B：Oh, they are our shoes. What do you expect me to do?

A：I want to change my shoes from Size 37 to Size 36.

B：___4___ I will exchange them for you at once.

A：It's kind of you, thank you.

B：___5___.

A. I'm sorry.   B. What's the matter?
C. You're welcome.   D. No problem.
E. Certainly, here you are.

四、场景模拟

编写一组对话,就某个问题进行投诉。

提示词汇：What's the problem/Would like…have…refunded

Unit 4 Customer Service

Reading and Writing

一、用单词的适当形式填空

1. The barber _____ (收费,要价) me ten *yuan* for the haircut.
2. He was asked to _____ (担任) as an advertiser on the project.
3. I want to make a _____ (投诉) about your products.
4. Thank you for your _____ (耐心).
5. You should _____ (道歉) to her for what you said.
6. It _____ (amaze) me to hear that you were leaving.
7. Never have I seen such an _____ (interest) movie.
8. Each bike carries a ten-year _____ (guarantee).
9. They had their house _____ (paint) last month.
10. We haven't found a _____ (solution) to this thing. But I'm sure we are on the right track.

二、完形填空

The plane took off. A passenger needed a cup of water to take his medicine. An air hostess told him that she would bring him the __1__ soon. But the air hostess was __2__ busy that she forgot to bring him the water. __3__, the passenger couldn't take his medicine on time. About half an hour later, she hurried over to him with a cup of water, but he __4__ it.

In the following hours, each time she __5__ the passenger, she would ask him with a smile whether he needed help or not. But the passenger __6__ paid notice to her.

When it was time to get off the __7__, the passenger asked her to hand him the passengers booklet (留言簿), she was very __8__. She thought that he would __9__ bad words in it, but with a smile she handed it to him.

Off the plane, she opened the booklet and then __10__. The passenger put it, "In the past few hours, you have asked me whether I needed help or not twelve times in all. How can I refuse your twelve faithful smiles?"

(   ) 1. A. medicine   B. cup   C. water   D. coffee
(   ) 2. A. so   B. water   C. quite   D. very
(   ) 3. A. With her help   B. On the one hand

		C. As a result		D. To tell the truth		
(	)4.	A. drank	B. accepted	C. received	D. refused
(	)5.	A. looked at	B. listened to	C. talked about	D. passed by
(	)6.	A. usually	B. never	C. sometimes	D. often
(	)7.	A. bus	B. train	C. ship	D. plane
(	)8.	A. sad	B. happy	C. excited	D. interested
(	)9.	A. break down	B. get down	C. write down	D. go down
(	)10.	A. laughed	B. smiled	C. wondered	D. worried

三、阅读理解

阅读下面短文，从每题所给的 A、B、C、D 四个选项中选出最佳答案。

136 Crestview Circle

Dover, Connecticut

January 16, 2021

Gander's Furniture Store

Stamford, Connecticut, 09876

Dear sir,

I am writing about your January bill, which I am returning with this letter. I am not going to pay this bill. Last month I bought a table and four chairs for $65.50. They were sent to me on December 18. That night one leg of the table broke while my wife was putting our dinner on it. It fell on one of the chairs, and that broke, too. Our $2.50 steak landed on the floor, and the dog ate it.

I spoke to the salesman who had sold me the table and the chairs. He told me to write you a letter. I wrote you on December 20, saying that I was not going to pay for the furniture. On December 21 some men came and took it back to the store.

Please do something about your records. I do not want to receive another bill for the furniture which I returned.

Yours truly,

Albert Robbins

(　　)1. From the letter we can conclude that Mr. Robbins had actually paid _____ for the table and the four chairs.

A. $65.50　　B. no money　　C. $2.50　　D. $68

(　　)2. Why do you think Mr. Robbins write the letter to the furniture store?

A. Because he had paid for the furniture but was asked to pay again.

B. Because he wanted the manager to scold the salesman for the bad furniture.

C. Because the furniture he bought was badly made and he wanted to return it.

D. Because he didn't want to receive a second bill for the furniture he had returned.

(　　)3. When did Mr. Robbins buy the furniture?

  A. Before December 18.   B. On December 20.

  C. On December 21.   D. On January 16.

(　　)4. What is Mr. Robbins' mood when he was writing the letter?

  A. He was anxious.   B. He was disappointed.

  C. He was angry.   D. He was friendly.

(　　)5. What did Mr. Robbins buy?

  A. A table and a chair.   B. A table and 4 chairs.

  C. A table.   D. A chair.

四、书面表达

给淘宝店主写一封投诉信,诉说你的不愉快购物经历,希望他们给出合理的答复。

_____

_____

_____

_____

Grammar

一、从下面每小题四个选项中选出最佳选项

(　　)1. It is three weeks _____ he worked here.

  A. before   B. since   C. after   D. while

(　　)2. We will go camping if it _____ tomorrow.

  A. hasn't rained   B. didn't rain

  C. doesn't rain   D. won't rain

(　　)3. This is _____ important a meeting _____ you should attend it.

  A. so, that   B. such, that   C. so, as to   D. though, that

( )4. I said nothing about it _____ his wife was there.
   A. however   B. because   C. so that   D. when

( )5. _____ you say I believe you.
   A. However   B. Whenever   C. Whichever   D. Whatever

( )6. _____ he is poor, she loves him.
   A. Even if   B. As if   C. Since   D. Unless

( )7. The house is _____ that one.
   A. three times as big as   B. three times as bigger as
   C. three times bigger than   D. three times more than

( )8. _____ you study harder, you will never pass the final exam.
   A. If   B. Unless   C. That   D. Since

( )9. _____ he can go to school by himself.
   A. As he is young   B. Young although he is
   C. Young as he is   D. Like he is young

( )10. _____ the sky is clear, you can see as far as the old temple on top of the mountain, but not today.
   A. When   B. Where   C. Though   D. Because

( )11. _____ you stick to it, you will succeed in the end.
   A. As far as   B. As long as   C. As well as   D. As good as

( )12. I was so familiar with him that I recognized his voice _____ I pick up the phone.
   A. while   B. after   C. in case   D. the minute

( )13. The _____ you study, the _____ progress you will make in English.
   A. hard, great   B. harder, greater
   C. hardest, greatest   D. hardly, greatly

( )14. The earth runs around the sun _____ the moon runs around the earth.
   A. as if   B. as though   C. just as   D. just like

( )15. —Your English is so good, how long have you been in England?
   —_____ I was 8.
   A. Until   B. Since   C. When   D. While

( )16. I'm tired _____ I don't have a rest for the whole day.
   A. or   B. because   C. but   D. so

( )17. Don't forget to turn off the lights _____ you leave.
   A. before   B. until   C. when   D. while

( )18. _____ I got to the classroom, all the students are reading the text.
　　　　A. Though　　B. Because　　C. If　　　　D. When

( )19. We won't reach the agreement with them _____ they obey the game rules.
　　　　A. if　　　　B. unless　　　C. when　　　D. once

( )20. It is 20 years _____ the swimming club was founded.
　　　　A. since　　　B. after　　　 C. before　　 D. when

( )21. Lucy worked late into the night _____ she could finish writing the papers.
　　　　A. such that　B. in order that　C. in order to　D. so as to

( )22. _____ it was very hot yesterday, he worked on the farm as usual.
　　　　A. Because　　B. For　　　　C. But　　　　D. Although

( )23. We will work _____ we are needed.
　　　　A. whenever　B. because　　C. wherever　　D. since

( )24. We always sing _____ we walk.
　　　　A. as　　　　B. since　　　C. but　　　　D. because

( )25. Hurry up, _____ you will be late.
　　　　A. and　　　B. but　　　　C. or　　　　　D. because

( )26. I will tell you _____ I get to Shanghai.
　　　　A. so　　　　B. as soon as　C. because　　D. though

( )27. Please remind me of the meeting tomorrow _____ I forget it.
　　　　A. as though　B. even though　C. in case　　D. so that

( )28. I was reading _____ my brother was playing games at this time yesterday.
　　　　A. as soon as　B. after　　　C. until　　　D. while

( )29. You'd better be more careful _____ you made a mistake.
　　　　A. when　　　B. why　　　　C. where　　　D. that

( )30. Tom knew nothing about it _____ his sister told him.
　　　　A. since　　　B. if　　　　 C. until　　　 D. after

二、找出下列句子中错误的选项，并改正过来

1. Because it was raining, so we stayed at home.
　　　A　　B　　　C　　　　D

2. The teacher treats me as if I am her child.
　　　　　　　A　　　B　　C　　D

3. Although it is dangerous, but I will try.
　　　A　　　B　　　　　C　D

4. He will go to see a film tomorrow if he will finish his homework.
　　　A　　　　　　　　　　　B　　C　　　D

5. I will eat no matter what you give me.
   A   B   C   D

6. No sooner has he arrived than he began to cry.
   A   B   C   D

7. The book is such interesting that I would like to read it again.
           A   B   C   D

8. It won't be long before he will catch up with us.
   A   B   C   D

9. It is so a heavy stone that I can't lift it up.
    A   B   C   D

10. The little boy saved every coin such that he could buy his mother a present on Mother's
               A   B   C   D
    Day.

1.（　）应为_____　　2.（　）应为_____　　3.（　）应为_____

4.（　）应为_____　　5.（　）应为_____　　6.（　）应为_____

7.（　）应为_____　　8.（　）应为_____　　9.（　）应为_____

10.（　）应为_____

For Better Performance

一、找出与所给单词画线部分读音相同的选项

（　）1. exchange   A. express   B. exam   C. exactly   D. example

（　）2. mention   A. question   B. suggestion   C. ingestion   D. relation

（　）3. patience   A. damage   B. location   C. apply   D. disaster

（　）4. promise   A. mobile   B. bright   C. risk   D. festival

（　）5. receipt   A. reduce   B. education   C. appreciate   D. expect

二、英汉互译

1. at the beginning of _____   2. for example _____

3. decide to do _____   4. on time _____

5. as quickly as possible _____   6. try one's best to do sth. _____

7. 道歉 _____   8. 安排做某事 _____

9. 归还 _____   10. 调换 _____

11. 在保修期 _____   12. 承诺 _____

三、用单词的适当形式填空

1. I agree to the _____（安排）about the birthday party.
2. They _____（推迟）their wedding because of the bad weather.
3. With many things to _____（处理）, I have to stop listening to the light music.
4. He didn't study hard, as a _____（结果）, he failed the final exam.
5. He won't come _____（除非）he is invited.
6. When _____（mention）AI, most of people are learning about it.
7. Improper investments cause great _____（loss）to the investors.
8. I saw the goods _____（deliver）to owners.
9. Could you please _____（exchange）the dress for me?
10. First of all, I want to express my _____（sincerely）apology for the delayed delivery.

四、找出下列句子中错误的选项，并改正过来

1. No matter <u>what</u> <u>successful</u> you are, you <u>should</u> never <u>look down upon</u> your co-workers.
         A   B   C   D

2. <u>At</u> the <u>begin</u> of English class, we all <u>say</u> "hello" <u>to</u> our teacher.
   A   B   C   D

3. <u>The</u> accident that <u>happened</u> yesterday <u>was</u> <u>due of</u> drunk driving.
  A   B   C   D

4. The camera <u>is</u> <u>such</u> expensive <u>that</u> I can't <u>afford</u> it.
            A B   C   D

5. <u>Poor</u> <u>as if</u> <u>I am</u>, I <u>din't</u> steal the money.
   A   B   C   D

1.( ) 应为_____   2.( ) 应为_____   3.( ) 应为_____

4.( ) 应为_____   5.( ) 应为_____

单元检测

第一部分 英语知识运用（共分三节，满分40分）

第一节 语音知识：从 A、B、C、D 四个选项中找出其画线部分与所给单词画线部分读音相同的选项。（共5分，每小题1分）

( ) 1. s<u>o</u>lution   A. symb<u>o</u>l   B. kn<u>o</u>ck   C. sh<u>o</u>t   D. j<u>o</u>b

( ) 2. ref<u>u</u>nd   A. red<u>u</u>ce   B. bea<u>u</u>ty   C. m<u>u</u>st   D. attit<u>u</u>de

(   )3. sport   A. work   B. doctor   C. director   D. lord
(   )4. delivery   A. lifestyle   B. battery   C. sky   D. apply
(   )5. cause   A. laugh   B. aunt   C. fault   D. because

第二节 词汇与语法知识：从 A、B、C、D 四个选项中选出可以填入空白处的最佳选项。(共 25 分，每小题 1 分)

(   )6. Tom always prefer _____ rather than _____.
   A. walk, ride   B. walk, reading
   C. to walk, ride   D. walking, riding

(   )7. Neither he nor I _____ from Canada, we are from China.
   A. is   B. are   C. be   D. am

(   )8. Though he is in his sixties _____, he still works as hard as a young man.
   A. yet   B. but   C. and   D. although

(   )9. Not you but your father _____ blame.
   A. is to   B. are to   C. be to   D. to be

(   )10. He is a hard-working student and he is sure _____ his English greatly in a short time.
   A. improving   B. improved   C. to improve   D. improves

(   )11. Would you please _____ the gifts for me?
   A. to open   B. open   C. opening   D. opened

(   )12. It is no good _____ so you'd better give it up.
   A. smoke   B. smoked   C. smoking   D. to smoke

(   )13. You should apologize _____ your sister _____ not telling her the truth.
   A. to, for   B. to, to   C. for; for   D. for; to

(   )14. Why not _____ a new way to do it?
   A. to try   B. trying   C. tried   D. try

(   )15. A seed can't decide _____ become a big tree _____ become food.
   A. if to, or to   B. whether to, or
   C. whether to, or to   D. if to, or

(   )16. Your teacher will be satisfied with you _____ you finish your homework on time.
   A. unless   B. as long as   C. as if   D. but

(   )17. The accident was _____ his carelessness.
   A. due to   B. because   C. thank to   D. as a result

(   )18. For the boy _____ above, nothing on earth can be _____ than his father's love.

A. mentioning, much valuable   B. mentioned, much valuable
C. mentioning, more valuable   D. mentioned, more valuable

( ) 19. All the students were _____ when they heard the _____ news.
A. excited, excited   B. excited, exciting
C. exciting, exciting   D. exciting, excited

( ) 20. Please _____ my sincere wishes for you and your family.
A. accepting   B. receive   C. accept   D. receiving

( ) 21. I must say sorry for any _____ caused by our company.
A. inconvenience   B. inconvenient
C. convenience   D. convenient

( ) 22. Because the sports watch is still _____ guarantee, I'll exchange a new one for your.
A. in   B. on   C. under   D. to

( ) 23. I'd like to have the computer _____.
A. to refund   B. refunded   C. refunding   D. being refunded

( ) 24. I will call you immediately _____ I get to your city.
A. as well as   B. as long as   C. as good as   D. as soon as

( ) 25. The price of this car has reduced _____ 15% this year because of the epidemic.
A. to   B. by   C. with   D. in

( ) 26. Secretary Gu is _____ everything in our school.
A. in charge   B. in charge of   C. in the charge of   D. with charge of

( ) 27. We will have to finish the work _____.
A. no matter long it takes   B. it takes however long
C. no matter how long it will take   D. however long it takes

( ) 28. He walked _____ fast _____ I couldn't follow him.
A. so, that   B. such, that   C. so that   D. such that

( ) 29. People who often stay up too late are more likely to die of heart disease _____ study.
A. with the help of   B. because of
C. according to   D. as a result

( ) 30. _____ he returns to his native land.
A. It is long before that   B. It is before long
C. It won't be long before   D. It will be long before that

第三节 完形填空：阅读下面的短文，从所给的 A、B、C、D 四个选项中选出正确的答案。（共 10 分，每小题 1 分）

A

When you are a teenager, it seems that every time you say to your parents, "I want to", your parents answer, "No, you can't" or "You can't do."

Young people further complain that their parents do not ___31___ them. When something goes wrong, most parents just don't believe in their children. ___32___ asking why, they think their kids are wrong. And not many parents allow their children to make a decision for ___33___.

Yes, ___34___ is true that your parents always treat you as a little child. You aren't allowed to do what you like. But remember that not long ago you were really a child. Your parents still remember the childish ___35___ you used to make. They want to protect you ___36___ you don't want them to do so.

So, if you want to get ___37___ freedom, please try to understand your parents and don't lie to them. Try a more friendly way. If you want them to ___38___ you to stay out late, don't just say, "All ___39___ kids in my class can stay out late." Tell them as much as you can about what you want to do and where you will be and ___40___ it is important for you to stay out late. Then they will say, "Yes, but be more careful and give us a call if possible."

( ) 31. A. enjoy　　　　B. prefer　　　　C. decide　　　　D. understand
( ) 32. A. Except　　　B. Instead　　　　C. Without　　　　D. With
( ) 33. A. themselves　B. their　　　　　C. they　　　　　　D. theirs
( ) 34. A. this　　　　　B. it　　　　　　　C. that　　　　　　D. one
( ) 35. A. uses　　　　　B. differences　　C. because　　　　D. mistakes
( ) 36. A. though　　　B. if　　　　　　　C. because　　　　D. since
( ) 37. A. more　　　　B. least　　　　　C. most　　　　　　D. less
( ) 38. A. hope　　　　B. allow　　　　　C. wish　　　　　　D. ask
( ) 39. A. another　　　B. others　　　　　C. the other　　　　D. the others
( ) 40. A. which　　　　B. what　　　　　C. when　　　　　　D. why

第二部分 篇章与词汇理解（共分三节 满分 50 分）

第一节 阅读理解：阅读下列短文，从每题所给的 A、B、C、D 四个选项中，选出最恰当的答案。（共 30 分，每小题 2 分）

A

When a consumer finds that an item she or he bought is faulty or in some other way does not

Unit 4 Customer Service

live up to the manufacturer's claims(制造商的说明), the first step is to present the warranty(保证), or any other records which might help, at the store of purchase. In most cases, this action will produce results. However, if it does not, there are various means the consumer may use to gain satisfaction. A simple and common method used by many consumers is to complain directly to the store manager. In general, the "higher up" his or her complaint, the faster he or she can expect it to be settled. In such a case, it is usually settled in the consumer's favor, assuming he or she has a just claim. Consumers should complain in person whenever possible, but if they cannot get to the place of purchase, it is acceptable to phone or write the complaint in a letter.

Complaining is usually most effective when it is done politely but firmly, and especially when the consumer can demonstrate what is wrong with the item in question. If this cannot be done, the consumer will succeed best by presenting specific information as to what is wrong, rather than by making general statements. For example, "The left speaker does not work at all and the sound coming out of the right one is unclear" is better than "This stereo does not work". The store manager may advise the consumer to write to the manufacturer. If so, the consumer should do this, stating the complaint as politely and firmly as possible. If a polite complaint does not achieve the desired result, the consumer can go to a step further. She or he can threaten to take the seller to court or report the seller to a private or public organization responsible for protecting consumer's rights.

(   )41. When a consumer finds that an item she or he bought is faulty, the first thing he or she should do is to _____.

   A. show some written proof of the purchase to the store

   B. threaten to take the matter to court

   C. write a firm letter of complaint to the store of purchase

   D. complain personally to the manager

(   )42. How can a consumer make his or her complaint more effective, according to the passage?

   A. Threaten to take the seller to court.

   B. Explain exactly what is wrong with the item.

   C. Make polite and general statements about the problem.

   D. Avoid having direct contact with the store manager.

(   )43. According to the passage, which of the following is suggested as the last alternative that consumers may turn to?

   A. Complain to the store manager in person.

   B. Complain to the manufacturer.

C. Write a complaint letter to the manager.

D. Turn to the Consumers' Rights Protection Organization for help.

(   )44. The underlined phrase "live up to" in this context means _____.

A. keep the promise of   B. realize the purpose of

C. fulfill the demands of   D. meet the standard of

(   )45. The passage tells us _____.

A. how to settle a consumer's complaint about a faulty item

B. how to avoid buying a faulty item

C. how to make an effective complaint about a faulty item

D. how to deal with complaints from customers

B

Tour Guides Wanted Two years' working experience. Good English and good at talking to people. Age: 20-30. Go to Friendship Traveling Company to ask the manager for more information.	Taxi Drivers Wanted Full-time taxi drivers. Over five years' experience, good knowledge of the city. Under 45 years old. For more information, please come to Shunda Taxi Company to visit the manger.
English Teachers Wanted Warm and patient college students. Able to speak standard English. Good with children. Time: on weekends. E-mail address: sunshineschool@163.com	Postmen Wanted No experience necessary but you must be hard-working. Free to choose working hours. Have a driver's license. Write to No. 38 Changhong Rd., Xiangyang.

(   )46. You can't get information by _____ if you want to get a job above.

A. making a call   B. going to visit the manager

C. sending an e-mail   D. writing a letter

(   )47. Sunshine School needs _____.

A. an outgoing tour guide   B. a hard-working postman

C. full-time drivers   D. excellent English teachers

(   )48. If you want to be a taxi driver, you should _____.

A. be over 45 years old   B. know the city very well

C. write to No. 38 Changhong Road   D. speak English well

(   )49. The tour guides wanted should _____.

      A. have no working experience   B. be patient with children

      C. speak good English   D. be good at driving

(   )50. If you want to be a postman, it's necessary for you to have _____.

      A. working experience   B. good knowledge of the city

      C. a driver's license   D. a college student card

C

    Everybody has to buy or sell things sometimes. Even students who are usually not very rich, have to learn something about making purchases intelligently. As a student, you may find, for example, that you need to a walkman or winter clothing. You may want to buy a television or a used car. Of course, you want to get good value for your money. If you are considering a major purchase, or any purchase you should remember several important things.

    Ⅰ. Study first, and then decide what you want to buy. You can learn a lot just by reading books, and advertisements.

    Remember that a high quality product will probably last longer and work better. Of course for a superior(优良的) product you are expected to pay more. An inferior product may not give you good quality, but the price should be low. Perhaps this seems obvious, but you know the quality Don't just look at the price. A poor quality product could be expensive. And a valuable one could is on sale at a greatly reduced price.

    Ⅱ. Don't hurry. Take your time. After you decide what product you want, go to many different stores. If you cannot find the product you want, you may try to order it directly form the factory or ask the store to order it for you.

    Look for a good deal(有利的交易). If you wait, you will probably find that your product will go on sale and you may be able to save 10, 20, or even 50 percent of the original price.

    Ⅲ. Finally, before you buy, make sure that the product is guaranteed(质量保证). If you find the lowest possible price, you will generally be happy with your purchase and also keep more money in the bank.

(   )51. If you cannot find things you plan to buy in the stores, you may _____.

      A. place an order directly with the factory

      B. wait until they arrive

      C. go to a bank to save money

      D. get angry with the salesman

( )52. You can get _____ by reading books and advertisements.

　　　A. something about the amount of product

　　　B. message of process

　　　C. facts of property

　　　D. information about products

( )53. It is dangerous _____ by its price alone.

　　　A. to deal with a product　　　B. to judge a product

　　　C. to use a product　　　　　D. to discuss a product

( )54. While you go shopping, you should pay more attention to _____.

　　　A. information　B. intelligence　　C. quality　　　D. price

( )55. Which of the following is the best title for this passage?

　　　A. What products can you choose.

　　　B. Do shopping wisely as a student.

　　　C. Take your time when shopping

　　　D. What can you do to save your money.

第二节　词义搭配：从(B)栏中选出(A)栏单词的正确解释。(共10分,每小题1分)

　　　　　　A　　　　　　　　　　　　B

( )56. exchange　　　　A. to take something somewhere

( )57. delay　　　　　 B. give somebody their money back

( )58. leaflet　　　　　C. give something to somebody and at the same time receive

　　　　　　　　　　　　something from others

( )59. refund　　　　　D. make…happen later

( )60. deliver　　　　　E. a piece of paper for writing or printing on

( )61. due to　　　　　F. say sorry to

( )62. charge　　　　　G. refer to

( )63. apologize　　　　H. ask somebody to do sth

( )64. mention　　　　 I. because of

( )65. request　　　　　J. in response of

第三节　补全对话：根据对话内容,从对话后的选项中选出能填入空白处的最佳选项。(共10分,每小题2分)

A: Good morning.

B: Morning, how can I do for you?

A: ___66___.

B：Oh, are you satisfied with them?

A：__67__.

B：There could have been some mistake. I apologize. I'll check it right now, __68__.

A：__69__.

B：Sorry, we can't refunded it. Because of the weather, the transportation time is too long, __70__.

A：OK. Thank you for your patience.

> A. No, I want to have them refunded and have my money back.
> B. Please wait for a moment.
> C. No problem.
> D. but we'll send another box for you, is that OK?
> E. Today I received the oranges which I bought in your shop four days ago.

第三部分　语言技能运用(共分四节　满分30分)

第一节　单词拼写：根据下列句子及所给汉语注释，在横线上写出该单词。(共5分，每小题1分)

71. Supermarkets can reasonably return and _____ (交换) goods.

72. I managed to find a _____ (解决方法) to the problem.

73. The young mother lost her _____ (耐心) because of the baby crying and crying.

74. When you buy something important, you'd better keep the _____ (收据) for a long time.

75. Please fill in the _____ (空白处) with the proper words.

第二节　词形变换：用括号内单词的适当形式填空，将正确答案写在横线上。(共5分，每小题1分)

76. Gas cars are more _____ (convenience) to power up.

77. We'll try our best to deliver the _____ (good) on time.

78. The careless waiter receives _____ (complaint) every day.

79. My electric car must be _____ (charge) every three days.

80. _____ (check) your text-paper carefully before you hand it in.

第三节　改错：从 A、B、C、D 四个画线处找出一处错误的选项，并写出正确答案。(共10分，每小题2分)

81. Only by practicing a few hours every day, you will be able to master the language.
　　　A　　　　　B　　　　　　　　　　　　　C　　　　　D

82. We must study hard in order that make our country much stronger.
　　　　　　　　　A　　　　　B　　C　　　　　　　　D

83. As a lot of trees have cut down, birds have no place to build their homes.
　　A　　　　　　　　B　　　　　　　　　C　　　　　　D

84. Because her excellent work, she was given many awards.
　　A　　　　　　B　　　　C　　　　D

85. The problem mentioning at the meeting will be solved soon.
　　　　　　　A　　B　　　　　　　C　　D

81. (　) 应为 _____　　82. (　) 应为 _____　　83. (　) 应为 _____

84. (　) 应为 _____　　85. (　) 应为 _____

第四节　书面表达 (共 10 分)

假设你是淘宝店主, 针对顾客的投诉, 写一封回信, 给出合理的答复。

Unit 5

Natural Wonders in the World

Warming-up

一、句型汇总

1. Do you want to climb to the top to see the wonders yourself someday? 你想有一天自己爬到山顶去看奇迹吗?

2. It's a flat-topped mountain that looks like a table. 这是一座平顶山,看起来像一张桌子。

3. The local people say that the cloud was formed from a contest between the devil and a local pirate a long time ago. 当地人说云是很久以前魔鬼和当地海盗之间的较量形成的。

4. The cloud of smoke they left became Table Mountain's table cloth. 他们留下的烟云变成了桌山的桌布。

5. Many visitors say this is the most special mountain they have ever seen. 很多参加者说这是他们见过的最特别的山。

6. As one of…, it attracts many travelers every year. 作为……之一,它每年吸引了很多游客。

7. There are small waterfalls inside the cave. 洞内有一些小瀑布。

8. What a happy family! 多么幸福的家庭呀!

9. This place is famous for its lifelike stones. 这个地方是因为它栩栩如生的石头出名的。

10. It is the longest rift in the world and can be seen from space. 它是世界上最长的裂缝,并能从太空上被看见。

11. These 20-50 meters high stones look like a forest from a distance. 这些20~50米高的石头从远处看像森林。

12. We have visited many waterfalls, and the Iguacu Falls are the most beautiful and powerful waterfalls we've ever seen. 我们已参观了很多瀑布，伊瓜苏瀑布是我们曾经见过的最美丽和强大的瀑布。

二、英汉互译

1. attract _____   2. figure _____
3. interview _____   4. lifelike _____
5. travel agency _____   6. 目的地 _____
7. 距离;远方 _____   8. 发现 _____
9. 印象深刻的 _____   10. 位于 _____
11. 独特的 _____   12. 根据 _____

Listening and Speaking

一、找出与所给单词画线部分读音相同的选项

(   ) 1. attr<u>a</u>ct   A. d<u>a</u>mage   B. <u>a</u>ttend   C. gr<u>a</u>sp   D. c<u>a</u>ke
(   ) 2. b<u>o</u>rder   A. supp<u>o</u>rt   B. d<u>o</u>ctor   C. w<u>o</u>rld   D. m<u>o</u>tor
(   ) 3. disc<u>o</u>ver   A. bl<u>o</u>ck   B. w<u>o</u>nder   C. l<u>o</u>cate   D. wr<u>o</u>ng
(   ) 4. r<u>i</u>ft   A. w<u>i</u>dth   B. p<u>i</u>rate   C. d<u>i</u>et   D. w<u>i</u>de
(   ) 5. t<u>ow</u>ering   A. fl<u>ow</u>   B. fl<u>ow</u>er   C. thr<u>ow</u>   D. gr<u>ow</u>

二、从B栏中找出与A栏中相对应的答语

A

1. Can I ask you some questions?
2. It has many great wonders, right?
3. Where is the Himalayas located?
4. Is it the tallest one in the world?
5. Have you ever been to Italy?

B

A. Yes, it really is.
B. Sure. It's my pleasure.
C. Yes, it has.
D. It's located in China.
E. No, I have never been to Italy.

Unit 5 Natural Wonders in the World

三、用所给句子补全下面对话

A：Hi！How was your summer vacation？

B： 1

A：Where did you go？

B：I went to Beijing with my parents.

A： 2

B：Lots of places，such as the Place Museum，the Forbidden City，the Imperial Palace，the Great Wall and so on.

A：Which place do you think is the most magnificent？

B： 3 How marvelous it is！

A： 4

B：It is one of the world's most famous wonders. I like it very much.

A：What is the total length of the Great Wall？

B： 5

A：Oh，really？ I can't wait to go there.

B：It is really worth visiting，you can go someday.

> A. Oh！It was great.
> B. It is more than 6，700 kilometers long.
> C. How do you like the Great Wall？
> D. What interesting places did you go there？
> E. I think it's the Great Wall.

四、场景模拟

编写一组对话，和你的朋友讨论一个自然奇观。

提示词汇：be located in/great wonders/travelers/natural/scenery

Reading and Writing

一、用单词的适当形式填空

1. They didn't reach the border _____ （目的地）until after dark.

2. _____ (距离) is not a problem on the Internet.

3. Can you _____ (预测) where the economy is heading?

4. There are many great _____ (奇观) in the world.

5. Did you hear the _____ (采访) with him on the radio?

6. She was an _____ (impress) teacher for me, her kindness to me impressed on my mind.

7. She is an extremely _____ (attract) girl, has a pitch-black hair.

8. The scientists show a recent _____ (discover) about human beings on TV.

9. There are _____ (vary) ways of solving problem.

10. He paced out the length and _____ (wide) of the classroom.

二、完形填空

In a small village in West Sumatra(苏门答腊岛), there is a special bridge. The 30-meter-long __1__ is not made of stones. It is made of tree roots(根). So people call it a __2__ bridge! Over one hundred years ago, students in this village had to go across a(n) __3__ and dangerous (危险的) bridge over the river to school. Then a __4__ named Pakih Sohan wanted to help his students. __5__ he saw some long tree roots along the river, he had an idea. He decided to use the __6__ on each side of the river to build a bridge. His work started in 1890. And it __7__ him over 26 years to make the bridge. The bridge becomes very __8__ as the tree roots grow. Today, the natural wonder(自然奇观) known as a living bridge has become a popular place for __9__ when you visit it some day, be sure to bring your __10__ with you. It's a great idea to take photos on the bridge. But on a rainy day, the bridge will become wet and slippery(滑的), so you should be careful.

( ) 1. A. village   B. bridge   C. city   D. house
( ) 2. A. living   B. jumping   C. running   D. standing
( ) 3. A. strong   B. nice   C. new   D. old
( ) 4. A. farmer   B. driver   C. teacher   D. singer
( ) 5. A. Before   B. If   C. When   D. So
( ) 6. A. tress   B. houses   C. hill   D. stones
( ) 7. A. cost   B. spent   C. gave   D. took
( ) 8. A. tall   B. strong   C. short   D. thin
( ) 9. A. dancers   B. students   C. tourists   D. workers
( ) 10. A. bag   B. camera   C. umbrella   D. pen

Unit 5　Natural Wonders in the World

三、阅读理解

阅读下面短文,从每题所给的 A、B、C、D 四个选项中选出最佳答案。

　　Kunming is the capital of Yunnan. It's a city with a long history. Kunming has a population of more than 5,000,000. Though the weather in Yunnan changes from place to place, Kunming is famous for her beautiful weather. It's neither too hot in summer nor too cold in winter. That's why more and more people like to travel and even to live here. You can see that great changes have taken place here. A lot of tall buildings, cinemas and hospitals have been put up. You can cross the streets over footbridges in the city. You can buy whatever you want in shops and supermarkets in or around the city. People's lives are becoming better and better.

　　At weekends or on holiday, people like to relax themselves in different places and in different ways. In winter, people, especially old people, would like to climb the Western Hills. From the top of the hills, you can have a good look at the beautiful scenery of Kunming. Far away from the hills, you can enjoy the Sleeping Beauty among the hills. After supper, families take a walk along the bank of Dianchi Lake. The Golden Temple and EXPO Garden(世博园) are two famous places of interest in the north of the city. EXPO Garden is known to people both at home and abroad. You can spend a whole day visiting the world-famous garden. A little farther away from the southeast of the city, a special forest welcomes you. It is not a tree forest, but a stone forest. So it is called the Stone Forest.

　　People in Kunming are very friendly. They often invite their friends home to try delicious food, like rice noodles. If you want to know more about Kunming and taste her food, please visit her yourself!

(　　)1. What's the population of Kunming?
　　　A. Over five thousand　　　　B. Over five million
　　　C. Over five billion　　　　　D. Over five hundred

(　　)2. The weather in Yunnan is _____.
　　　A. the same in different places　　B. neither too hot nor too cold
　　　C. different in different places　　D. different in the same place

(　　)3. The Sleeping Beauty is the name of a _____.
　　　A. person　　B. hill　　C. shop　　D. film star

(　　)4. _____ is known to people all over the world.
　　　A. EXPO Garden　　　　　　B. The Stone Forest
　　　C. The Golden Temple　　　　D. The Western Hills

(　　)5. The writer of this passage wants to _____.

A. taste her food B. visit Kunming
C. invite tourists to Kunming D. know more about Kunming

四、书面表达

以"Mountain Tai"为题,写一篇文章,字数 80~100 字。

_____
_____
_____
_____
_____

Grammar

一、从下面每小题四个选项中选出最佳选项

(　　) 1. He asked _____ for the computer.
A. did I pay how much B. I paid how much
C. how much did I pay D. how much I paid

(　　) 2. "Please close the window," he said to me.
→He _____ me _____ the window.
A. said to; to close B. told to; closing
C. asked ; to close D. said to; please close

(　　) 3. "Have you seen the film?" he asked me. →He asked me _____.
A. had I seen the film B. have I seen the film
C. if I have seen the film D. whether I had seen the film

(　　) 4. The girls asked if they _____ some food and drink with them.
A. took B. take C. takes D. will take

(　　) 5. Mary said that she _____ to Guangzhou.
A. has never gone B. had never gone
C. has never been D. had never been

(　　) 6. Could you tell me whether they _____ dictation today?
A. had B. has C. will have D. are

(　　) 7. She asked Linda if _____ go and get some water.

Unit 5 Natural Wonders in the World

  A. could she B. she could C. she can D. she may

(　　) 8. Linda said the moon _____ round the earth.

  A. traveled B. has traveled C. travels D. had traveled

(　　) 9. He asked me _____ with me.

  A. what the matter is B. what the mater was

  C. what's the matter D. what was the matter

(　　) 10. The young man asked _____ it's summer or winter.

  A. either B. that C. weather D. whether

(　　) 11. We don't know _____ they did it.

  A. how B. who C. what D. which

(　　) 12. The teacher asks us _____ Jim can come back on time.

  A. that B. if C. when D. what time

(　　) 13. Does anybody know _____ we will have a sports meeting this weekend or not.

  A. if B. where C. whether D. that

(　　) 14. I wonder _____ he is crying now.

  A. that B. why C. how D. when

(　　) 15. Have you found out _____ we can do on Hainan Island?

  A. what B. how C. if D. whether

(　　) 16. Lily said _____ she had finished her composition.

  A. if B. that C. when D. where

(　　) 17. I don't know _____ he still lives here.

  A. where B. what C. when D. whether

(　　) 18. Could you show me _____?

  A. how can I get to the station B. where is the station

  C. how I could get to the station D. how I can reach the station

(　　) 19. Please tell me _____.

  A. what does he like B. what he does like

  C. what he likes D. what he like

(　　) 20. My sister told him _____.

  A. what day was it B. when the train arrived

  C. who she was waiting D. where did you live

(　　) 21. Could you tell me where we _____ next week?

  A. would go B. to go

  C. had to go D. will go

( )22. Could you tell me how much _____ to fly to Hainan?
   A. do it cost   B. does it cost
   C. it cost   D. it costs

( )23. The small children don't know _____.
   A. what is their stockings in   B. what is in their stockings
   C. where is their stockings in   D. what in their stockings

( )24. Can you tell me _____ you were born, Betty?
   A. who   B. what   C. when   D. that

( )25. I don't know _____ they have passed the exam.
   A. what   B. if   C. when   D. where

( )26. I hardly understand _____ he has told me.
   A. that   B. what   C. which   D. who

( )27. He asked me _____ told me the accident.
   A. whom   B. which   C. who   D. whose

( )28. He asked his friend _____ to go there or not.
   A. if   B. whether   C. what   D. that

( )29. —I don't know _____ Mr. Green will come to see us.
     —He will help us with our English.
   A. why   B. when   C. how   D. where

( )30. —We never know _____ the old man is.
     —They say he is a teacher.
   A. what   B. who   C. which   D. where

二、找出下列句子中错误的选项，并改正过来

1. This is the factory where we visited last night.
      A   B   C   D

2. Can you tell me how can I get to the nearest post office?
     A   B   C   D

3. Could you please tell me what the restrooms are?
       A   B   C   D

4. I didn't know when the plane was late.
      A   B   C D

5. I am not sure if he will come or not.
    A   B   C   D

6. He told me that he has been to Shanghai twice.
      A   B   C   D

Unit 5　Natural Wonders in the World

7. Could you tell me how he went to school every day?
　　A　　　B　　　　　　C　　　　　D

8. He said three quarters of the earth was covered with water.
　　　A　　　B　　　　　　　　C　　　　D

9. He asked me when the meeting will begin?
　　　A　　　B　　　　　　　　C　　D

10. We know what we should learn from each other.
　　　A　　B　　　　　C　　　　D

1. (　) 应为_____　　2. (　) 应为_____　　3. (　) 应为_____
4. (　) 应为_____　　5. (　) 应为_____　　6. (　) 应为_____
7. (　) 应为_____　　8. (　) 应为_____　　9. (　) 应为_____
10. (　) 应为_____

For Better Performance

一、找出与所给单词画线部分读音相同的选项

(　) 1. taste　　　A. rather　　B. handshake　　C. facial　　D. admit

(　) 2. explain　　A. example　　B. exit　　C. excuse　　D. expert

(　) 3. rude　　　A. suggest　　B. jump　　C. include　　D. useful

(　) 4. leave　　　A. bread　　B. break　　C. area　　D. mean

(　) 5. rather　　A. thank　　B. gather　　C. thick　　D. think

二、英汉互译

1. natural wonders _____　　2. list reasons _____

3. amazing _____　　　　　4. travel destinations _____

5. develop into _____　　　　6. look like _____

7. 向……介绍 _____　　　　8. 作为……出名 _____

9. 两者之间 _____　　　　　10. 从……到…… _____

11. 被当作 _____　　　　　12. 充满 _____

三、用单词的适当形式填空

1. What's the total _____ (long) of the Yellow River.

2. Her performance made a strong _____ (impress) on the audience.

3. He once told an _____ (interview) that he didn't like pop music.

— 81 —

4. This is a _____ (wonder) place for a picnic.

5. The population in China is much _____ (large) than that in Japan.

6. The Great Wall attracts thousands of _____ (游客) every year.

7. In the distance loomed a _____ (高耸的) mountain.

8. The horse he painted is very _____ (逼真的).

9. They didn't reach the _____ (边界) until after dark.

10. I have been picked out to _____ (代表) the whole team.

四、找出下列句子中错误的选项,并改正过来

1. There is nothing which you can do for me.
      A   B   C   D

2. The teacher asks him what he was doing at seven yesterday.
            A   B   C   D

3. I don't know that they will hold a party tonight.
       A   B   C   D

4. Great changes had taken place in our village since 2000.
      A   B   C   D

5. Mao Buyi is known for a famous singer.
       A   B C   D

1.( ) 应为_____   2.( ) 应为_____   3.( ) 应为_____

4.( ) 应为_____   5.( ) 应为_____

单元检测

第一部分　英语知识运用(共分三节,满分40分)

第一节　语音知识:从 A、B、C、D 四个选项中找出其画线部分与所给单词画线部分读音相同的选项。(共5分,每小题1分)

(　　)1. cancer　　A. attack　　B. place　　C. relax　　D. around

(　　)2. vary　　　A. yesterday　B. healthy　C. apply　　D. reply

(　　)3. rift　　　A. realize　　B. attitude　C. advertise　D. smile

(　　)4. believe　　A. lie　　　　B. friend　　C. field　　　D. society

(　　)5. smooth　　A. weather　　B. through　C. youth　　D. third

Unit 5　Natural Wonders in the World

第二节　词汇与语法知识：从 A、B、C、D 四个选项中选出可以填入空白处的最佳选项。（共 25 分，每小题 1 分）

(　　)6. Can you see the white cloud _____ the mountain?
　　A. on　　　　　B. above　　　　C. with　　　　D. near

(　　)7. It is also _____ that there's a story about "tablecloth".
　　A. saying　　　B. said　　　　　C. says　　　　D. to say

(　　)8. The falls are 1.7 miles long and rang _____ 197 _____ 269 feet high.
　　A. from; with　B. from; on　　　C. /; to　　　　D. from; to

(　　)9. The reef is located _____ the Coral Sea, off the coast _____ Queensland, Australia.
　　A. in; of　　　B. on; to　　　　C. to; of　　　　D. /; of

(　　)10. It is known _____ one of the seven natural wonders of the world.
　　A. for　　　　B. as　　　　　　C. to　　　　　D. about

(　　)11. The Stone Forest finally developed _____ different shapes, such as plants, animals and human beings.
　　A. into　　　　B. to　　　　　　C. of　　　　　D. with

(　　)12. A lot of people _____ to the party were famous.
　　A. inviting　　B. invited　　　　C. being invited　　D. invite

(　　)13. _____ role she played in the movie!
　　A. How moving　　　　　　　　B. How a moving
　　C. What moving　　　　　　　　D. What a moving

(　　)14. Do you remember the name of the company _____?
　　A. where she works at　　　　　B. for which she works in
　　C. in which she works　　　　　D. in where she works

(　　)15. He doesn't like _____.
　　A. what did his doctor say　　　B. that did his doctor say
　　C. what his doctor said　　　　D. that his doctor says

(　　)16. It is reported that _____ people die of lung cancer each year.
　　A. three thousands　　　　　　B. thousands of
　　C. thousand of　　　　　　　　D. three thousand of

(　　)17. —Do you play _____ football in your free time?
　　—No. I like music. I often play _____ violin.
　　A. /; the　　　B. /; /　　　　　C. the; the　　　D. the; /

(　　)18. He didn't go home _____ he finished his homework.

— 83 —

A. until　　　B. after　　　C. when　　　D. since

(　)19. It was _____ powerful cellphone that both of my friends decided to buy it.

　　A. so a　　　B. such a　　　C. a such　　　D. a so

(　)20. The reason _____ he was late was that he overslept.

　　A. because of　B. because　　C. why　　　D. that

(　)21. The fact _____ she works hard is well known to us all.

　　A. which　　B. whether　　C. what　　　D. that

(　)22. It's said that one fifth of Qin's population _____ to build the Great Wall.

　　A. forced　　B. had forced　　C. would be forced　D. were forced

(　)23. The young teacher is popular _____ her students.

　　A. for　　　B. at　　　C. with　　　D. from

(　)24. It was last summer _____ I saw him.

　　A. that　　　B. when　　　C. who　　　D. where

(　)25. His father _____ the Party since 1978.

　　A. joined　　B. has joined　　C. was in　　D. has been in

(　)26. Have you decided _____ on holiday?

　　A. go where　B. where to go　C. to go where　D. where go

(　)27. —Do you know Mary's grandpa?

　　—Of course. He is a kind old man, but he has _____ for about two years since he _____ in the accident.

　　A. been dead; was killed　　B. died; was killed

　　C. been dead; killed　　　　D. died; killed

(　)28. —I am very nervous, mom.

　　—_____, David!

　　A. Take it easy　B. Have fun　C. Take care　D. No problem

(　)29. It is reported _____ a space station will be built on the moon in years to come.

　　A. this　　　B. what　　　C. that　　　D. which

(　)30. It has been 10 years _____ I graduated from college.

　　A. when　　B. since　　　C. for　　　D. before

第三节　完形填空：阅读下面的短文，从所给的 A、B、C、D 四个选项中选出正确的答案。（共 10 分，每小题 1 分）

You don't need to spend lots of money on a vacation in Italy, because there are many　31　things to do and to see in Italy. Use these suggestions for free things to do　32　traveling in

Italy.

  33 is really the best way to see many of Italy's top sights and is free, so it's a great way to   34   time on your vacation. You can see a lot by just walking around, not spending a cent. Many cities and towns have pedestrian zones(步行街). If you're by the   35 , you'll usually find a seaside promenade(散步场所).

Florence, one of Italy's most popular tourist cities, holds many free sights for the   36 . Florence is a good city for walking and one of the best things to   37   in Florence is just walking around and watching the beautiful squares and buildings.

If you're ready to   38   the tourist crowds, go   39   the river on Ponte Vespucci (west of Ponte Vecchio) to the area known as Oltrarno. Here you'll   40   interesting neighborhoods that see fewer tourists. While there aren't any major monuments(纪念馆), the area is pleasant for hanging out and you'll see special Florentine buildings, shops and neighborhood squares.

( )31. A. good   B. interesting   C. free   D. expensive
( )32. A. where   B. when   C. what   D. how
( )33. A. Driving   B. Walking   C. Flying   D. Riding
( )34. A. cost   B. take   C. pay   D. spend
( )35. A. lake   B. sea   C. river   D. village
( )36. A. tourists   B. reporters   C. authors   D. students
( )37. A. see   B. hear   C. do   D. visit
( )38. A. take part in B. get away from   C. get on with   D. give away
( )39. A. across   B. through   C. over   D. on
( )40. A. look   B. watch   C. hear   D. find

第二部分　篇章与词汇理解(共分三节　满分50分)

第一节　阅读理解：阅读下列短文,从每题所给的 **A、B、C、D** 四个选项中,选出最恰当的答案。(共30分,每小题2分)

A

Hawaii is famous for its beautiful beaches. Every year water sports, especially surfing and water skiing attract many tourists to the island.

Hawaii has been a magical name to people who like to travel for many years. People on both sides of the Pacific Ocean(太平洋), in Japan and in America, dream of seeing these beautiful islands in the middle of the ocean. In the tropical(热带的) lands, the sun drops like a ball of golden fire into the sea, and it drops so quickly that you can not see it move. The sun leaves behind a glow(光辉) that lights the sky in the quiet water.

People often have a quiet, enjoyable time walking along the water. This scenery here is not very different from the exciting beauty that greeted the first tourists to these islands centuries ago. They came in canoes not much bigger than small boats.

They found the beautiful white sand beaches and the waving palm trees(棕榈树), but there were no grand hotels like the ones we see today. The first people came to Hawaii nearly two thousand years ago, but skyscraper(摩天大楼) hotels were only built in the last 25 years. Now planes make it possible to fly to Hawaii for a weekend from Tokyo or San Francisco.

No matter where people come from, they really want to see the earliest beauty of Hawaii. They want to see the lovely beaches and the mountains which are almost hidden by the tall hotels.

(   )41. What's Hawaii famous for?
A. The beautiful beaches.　　　　B. The tourists to the island.
C. The waving palm trees.　　　　D. Surfing and water skiing.

(   )42. What does the sun drop like in the tropical lands?
A. The sea.　　　　B. A ball of golden fire.
C. A glow.　　　　D. The quiet water.

(   )43. When did the first people come to Hawaii?
A. In 1987.　　　　B. About twenty-five years ago.
C. In 1012.　　　　D. About two thousand years ago.

(   )44. The beauty of the islands _____ for centuries.
A. has changed　　　　B. has greeted the first tourists
C. has remained nearly unchanged　D. has been the same

(   )45. Which is TRUE according to the passage?
A. People really want to see the earliest beauty of Hawaii.
B. People often have a quiet, unhappy time walking along the water.
C. People only in Japan dream of seeing the beautiful islands.
D. People found the beautiful red sand beaches in Hawaii.

B

Saturday, March 24th

We have arrived in the hot, wet city of Bangkok. This is our first trip to Thailand(泰国). All the different smells make us want to try the food. We are going to eat something special for dinner tonight. The hotel we are staying in is cheap, and very clean. We plan to stay here for a few days, visit some places in the city, and then travel to Chiang Mai in the north.

Tuesday, March 27th

Bangkok is wonderful and surprising. The places are interesting. We visited the famous market which was on water, and saw a lot of fruits and vegetables. Everything is so colorful, and we have taken hundreds of photos already! Later today we will leave for Chiang Mai. We will take the train north, stay in Chiang Mai for two days, and then catch a bus to Chiang Rai.

Friday, March 30th

Our trip to Chiang Rai was long and boring. We visited a small village in the mountains. The villagers here love the quiet life-no computers or phones. They are the kindest people I have ever met. They always smile and say "hello". Kathy and can only speak a few words of Thai, so smiling is the best way to show our kindness. I feel good here and hope to be able to come back next year.

( ) 46. The diaries above show the writer's _____ days in Thailand.
    A. three   B. seven   C. fifteen   D. twenty

( ) 47. It seems that visitors _____ in Bangkok.
    A. often feel hungry   B. can't take any photos
    C. can have a good time   D. don't feel interested

( ) 48. Which of the following is TRUE?
    A. Chiang Mai is a beautiful city in the south of Thailand.
    B. The writer left Chiang Mai for Chiang Rai by bus.
    C. The writer is traveling alone in Thailand.
    D. The trip to Chiang Rai was long but interesting.

( ) 49. The villagers _____.
    A. are friendly to others   B. like to speak English
    C. hope to live in cities   D. are bored of the peaceful life

( ) 50. What is the best title(标题) of the whole diary?
    A. My First Travel.   B. The Outside World.
    C. Traveling in Thailand.   D. Beautiful and Interesting Place.

C

This is a talk by a London taxi driver.

"I've been a taxi driver for nearly ten years. Most London taxi drivers have their own taxis." It's a nice job most of time. You meet a lot of people. I always work at night, because there is too much traffic during the day. I live twenty miles outside London and I go to work at 5:30 in the afternoon."

"I usually go home between 2 and 3 in the morning."

"Some very strange things happened late at night. The other day I was taking a woman home from a party. She had her little dog with her. When we got to her house, she found that she had lost her key. So I waited in the car with the dog while she climbed in through a window."

"I waited and waited. After half an hour of ringing the bell I decided to find out what was going on. I tied the dog to a tree and started to climb in through the window. The next thing I knew was that the police came. They thought I was a thief."

"Luckily the woman came downstairs(下楼). She must have gone to sleep and forgotten about me and the dog!"

(　　)51. The driver always worked at night because it was easier to _____.

   A. drive   B. make money

   C. climb in through the window   D. meet a lot of people

(　　)52. The woman climbed in through a window because _____.

   A. she wanted to have a sleep

   B. her husband didn't open the door for her

   C. she didn't want to pay the driver

   D. she couldn't find her key

(　　)53. The story happened _____.

   A. early in the morning   B. late at night

   C. 20 miles outside London   D. near a police station

(　　)54. Which of the following is wrong?

   A. The driver usually stops working between 2 and 3 in the morning.

   B. The police made a mistake.

   C. The woman had no money to pay the driver.

   D. The woman had forgotten about the driver and the dog.

(　　)55. The driver climbed in through the window to _____.

   A. get money from the woman

   B. return the dog to the woman

   C. see what was happening in the house

   D. phone the police

第二节　词义搭配：从(B)栏中选出(A)栏单词的正确解释。(共10分，每小题1分)

     A   B

(　　)56. ancient   A. knowledge shared by society

(　　)57. culture   B. in the old days

(　　)58. amazing   C. because of

(　　)59. construct   D. a large building in Egypt

(　　)60. expression   E. the person who do something frequently

Unit 5 Natural Wonders in the World

(   )61. interview   F. a look on a person's face that shows their thoughts or feelings

(   )62. regular   G. surprising

(   )63. pyramid   H. build

(   )64. due to   I. a meeting in which someone asks another person

(   )65. stretch   J. make something longer or wider; extend

第三节 补全对话：根据对话内容，从对话后的选项中选出能填入空白处的最佳选项。(共10分,每小题2分)

A：Hey, Excuse me. __66__

B：Yes, and you are…

A：__67__ This is my ID card(身份证), Would you please show me yours?

B：OK, Miss Li. __68__

A：Welcome to Beijing, Miss Wang. I'm so glad that the first one asked is the guest I will receive.

B：Thank you Miss Li. __69__

A：Let me help you with your luggage. Our car is waiting for us at the exit. __70__

B：Thank you very much for your good service.

A：It's a pleasure.

> A. I'm so lucky that I can meet my guide as soon as I get off the plane.
> B. I'm Miss Li, a guide from Beijing Travel service.
> C. Here you are.
> D. It will take us right to the hotel.
> E. Are you Miss Wang from Shanghai?

第三部分 语言技能运用(共分四节 满分30分)

第一节 单词拼写：根据下列句子及所给汉语注释，在横线上写出该单词。(共5分,每小题1分)

71. The _____ (距离) from Marathon to Athens was about 26 miles.

72. He went to the job _____ (面试) confidently.

73. Why not _____ (邀请) him to your journey?

74. In a way, knowledge is a kind of _____ (强有力的) arm.

75. He _____ (声称) to be a good scientist.

第二节 词形变换：用括号内单词的适当形式填空,将正确答案写在横线上。(共 5 分,每小题 1 分)

76. The _____ (differ) among seasons aren't obvious in this city.

77. I think at the beginning of each book a brief _____ (introduce) to it is necessary.

78. Huangshan is _____ (locate) in Anhui Province.

79. A visit to the museum is an _____ (forget) experience.

80. This mountain's _____ (beautiful) attracted many people.

第三节 改错：从 A、B、C、D 四个画线处找出一处错误的选项,并写出正确答案。(共 10 分,每小题 2 分)

81. How great wonders they are!
     A   B   C   D

82. She is interesting in the Chinese history.
     A   B   C   D

83. The Yangtza River is longer than any river in China.
                       A   B   C   D

84. He gave me a watch and said to me, "It can tell you what is the time."
        A   B   C   D

85. I never have seen such a person before.
      A   B   C   D

81. ( ) 应为 _____ 82. ( ) 应为 _____ 83. ( ) 应为 _____

84. ( ) 应为 _____ 85. ( ) 应为 _____

第四节 书面表达(共 10 分)

作文题目：The Imperial Mountain Summer Resort。

词数要求：80~100 词。

写作要点：介绍承德避暑山庄。(地理位置、历史、地位)

Unit 6

Living History of Culture

Warming-up

一、句型汇总

1. It has a history of... years. 它有……年的历史。

2. It is the starting point of... 它是……的起点。

3. It is the right place to learn about... 它是学习关于……的合适的地方。

4. It is just like a living history book. 它就像一本活生生的历史书。

5. Where did you go during the holiday? 你假期去了哪里?

6. Beijing has a history of more than 3,000 years. 北京有 3000 多年的历史。

7. It's the capital city of China and one of the most attractive places around the world. 它是中国的首都,并且是全世界最有吸引力的地方之一。

8. Like most tourists, the very first destination that I went to visit in Xi'an was the Terracotta Army. 像大多数的旅行者,我去参观西安的第一站是秦兵马俑。

9. The warriors are all life-sized and set in regular rows. 这些兵马俑都是真人大小,并且有规律的排列。

10. On the edge of the Sahara Desert lies the Great Pyramid of Giza, which was constructed for Egyptian King Khufu between 2600 and 2500. 吉萨大金字塔位于撒哈拉沙漠的边缘,它是

在公元前 2600 年到公元前 2500 年间为埃及国王胡夫建造的。

11. Just as every nation has a different culture, so do their eating habits. 就像每个国家都有不同的文化，他们的饮食习惯也一样。

12. In the United States, the days starts with quite a big breakfast. 在美国，一天以丰盛的早餐开始。

13. North Africans prefer their meals hearty and spicy. 北非人喜欢丰盛而辛辣的食物。

14. The Asian kitchen is considered one of the healthiest kitchens in the world, due to the amount of fish and vegetables. 亚洲厨房里有大量的鱼和蔬菜，因此被誉为世界上最健康的厨房之一。

二、英汉互译

1. amazingly _____
2. construction _____
3. fantastic _____
4. standing point of _____
5. on the edge of _____
6. 古代的 _____
7. 特别地 _____
8. 表情 _____
9. 有规律的 _____
10. 灰色的 _____
11. 丝绸之路 _____
12. 最初 _____

Listening and Speaking

一、找出与所给单词画线部分读音相同的选项

( ) 1. am<u>a</u>zingly A. n<u>a</u>tional B. <u>a</u>ward C. f<u>a</u>ntastic D. <u>a</u>dult

( ) 2. <u>ex</u>actly A. <u>ex</u>pression B. <u>ex</u>ample C. <u>ex</u>tend D. <u>ex</u>ercises

( ) 3. blo<u>ck</u> A. <u>c</u>ross B. <u>c</u>ontrol C. <u>c</u>onstruct D. stone

( ) 4. re<u>g</u>ular A. de<u>g</u>ree B. e<u>f</u>fect C. es<u>c</u>ape D. e<u>f</u>fort

( ) 5. stret<u>ch</u> A. s<u>ch</u>ool B. <u>ch</u>emical C. <u>ch</u>ange D. stoma<u>ch</u>

Unit 6 Living History of Culture

二、从B栏中找出与A栏中相对应的答语

A

1. Where did you go during the holiday?
2. What are they talking about?
3. Why are you interested in it?
4. Could you tell me more about it?
5. Which is the most attractive?

B

A. I went to Shanghai.
B. Because it is beautiful.
C. It must be the Great Wall!
D. No problem.
E. An interesting story book.

三、用所给句子补全下面对话

A：I hear that you have just been to Australia and New Zealand. Can you tell me something about the two countries?

B：___1___ You can leave a town and drive for hours before coming to the next one. There are more nationalities there. But New Zealand has a much cooler climate.

A：___2___

B：They both have beautiful beaches, green forests and mountains. So traveling in both countries is very exciting.

A：What about the cultures?

B：___3___ Perhaps because they are such close neighbors. Both cultures are very relaxed and friendly. You can go into a corner shop to buy a drink and then end up to talking to shop keeper for hours.

A：Can you say something more about it?

B：___4___

A：Thank you for telling me so much knowledge.

B：___5___

A. Well, Australia is much bigger than New Zealand.
B. People in both countries are sports mad.
C. Is there anything similar about them?
D. They have very similar cultures.
E. It's my pleasure.

四、场景模拟

编写一组对话,向你的朋友介绍大理。

提示词汇：be interested in/history/be located in/attractive/tourist

Reading and Writing

一、用单词的适当形式填空

1. Young people often congregate in the main _____ （广场）in the evenings.
2. This is a small _____ （极好的）supermarket nearby.
3. The beautiful little birds flying in the air are dressed in black and _____ （灰色的）.
4. This book over there is about _____ （古代的）.
5. As a student, we should have _____ （有规律的）eating habits.
6. This railway is still under _____ （construct）.
7. _____ （amazing）, they worked out how to do this successfully.
8. Amy loves all kinds of sports, _____ （especial）running.
9. There was no _____ （express）on her face.
10. _____ （origin）, we had intended to go to Italy, but then we won the trip to Greece.

二、完形填空

Several years ago, some students from the US visited our school. When we talked, I discovered __1__ differences in school life between the US and China. For example, each class __2__ fifty minutes in the US. It is a little __3__ than that in China. We usually have forty or fifty-five minutes in each class. Another difference is that they have less break time between __4__. Besides, although most schools in both countries finish their __5__ classes at 12 o'clock, the students in the US only have an hour-long break, so they __6__ eat lunch quickly. Their afternoon classes begin at 1:00 p.m. and school is over __7__ 3:00 p.m. Then they take part in club activities or play sports.

Many Chinese students don't work during their high school years, while the US students like to find a part-time job in __8__ free time. They don't have a dream job in mind. They think __9__ is no difference between jobs. Working is a useful experience for them and they can make money at the time. Some of them even take one-year full-time jobs __10__ they leave high school and then go to college.

( ) 1. A. no   B. few   C. little   D. some
( ) 2. A. lasts   B. finishes   C. starts   D. stays

Unit 6 Living History of Culture

(   )3. A. shorter   B. longer   C. earlier   D. later
(   )4. A. schools   B. classes   C. meals   D. students
(   )5. A. day   B. night   C. morning   D. afternoon
(   )6. A. can't   B. mustn't   C. need to   D. are able to
(   )7. A. in   B. for   C. during   D. around
(   )8. A. my   B. his   C. their   D. your
(   )9. A. it   B. there   C. that   D. this
(   )10. A. after   B. with   C. while   D. during

三、阅读理解

阅读下面短文,从每题所给的 A、B、C、D 四个选项中选出最佳答案。

Different countries have different customs. When you travel to other countries, please follow their customs, just as the saying goes, "_____"

Very often people who travel to the United States forget to tip(付小费). It is usual to tip porters who help carry your bags, taxi drivers and waiters. Waiters expect to get a 15% tip on the cost of your meal. Taxi drivers expect about the same amount. In England, make sure to stand in line even if there are only two of you. It's important to respect lines there. It's a good idea to talk about the weather. It's a favorite subject of conversation with the British.

In Spain, it's a good idea to have a light meal in the afternoon if someone invites you for dinner. People have dinner very late, and restaurants do not generally open until after 9 pm.

In Arab countries, men kiss one another on the cheek(脸颊). Your host may welcome you with a kiss on both cheeks. It is polite for you to do the same.

In Japan, people usually give personal or business cards to each other when they meet for the first time. When a person gives you a card, don't put it into your pocket right away. The person expects you to read it.

Don't forget to be careful of your body language to express something in conversation. A kind of body language that is acceptable in one culture may be impolite in another.

(   )1. When you travel to the USA, you don't need to tip _____.
　　A. porters   B. waiters   C. doctors   D. taxi drivers
(   )2. The missing sentence in the first paragraph should be "_____"
　　A. Love me, love my dog.
　　B. He who laughs last laughs best.
　　C. When in Rome, do as the Romans do.
　　D. Where there is a will, there is a way.

(　　)3. The underlined word "porters" in the passage means _____.

  A. 搬运工 B. 清洁工 C. 按线员 D. 售票员

(　　)4. Which of the following is TRUE according to the passage?

  A. In Spain, people usually have dinner very early.

  B. In England, it's not polite to talk about the weather.

  C. In Arab countries, men kiss one another on the cheek.

  D. In Japan, you should not read the business card as soon as you get it.

(　　)5. What's the best title of the passage?

  A. How to Tip. B. Body Language.

  C. When to Have Dinner. D. Advice to International Traveler.

四、书面表达

以"Welcome to Beijing"为题，写一篇文章，字数 80~100 字。

_____

_____

_____

_____

Grammar

一、从下面每小题四个选项中选出最佳选项

(　　)1. This is all _____ I know about the matter.

  A. that B. what C. who D. whether

(　　)2. Is there anything else _____ you require?

  A. which B. that C. who D. what

(　　)3. The last place _____ we visited was the Great Wall.

  A. which B. that C. where D. it

(　　)4. He talked happily about the men and books _____ interested him greatly in the school.

Unit 6 Living History of Culture

  A. which   B. that   C. it   D. whom

( ) 5. There is no dictionary _____ you can find everything.

  A. that   B. which   C. where   D. in that

( ) 6. This is one of the best books _____.

  A. that have ever been written   C. that has written

  B. that has ever been written   D. that have written

( ) 7. He wrote a letter to me, telling me everything _____ he saw on the way to Paris.

  A. what   B. that   C. which   D. where

( ) 8. Is oxygen the only gas _____ helps fire burn?

  A. that   B. /   C. which   D. it

( ) 9. Is there anything _____ to you?

  A. that is belonged   B. that belongs

  C. which belongs   D. that belong

( ) 10. The scientist and his achievements _____ you told me about are admired by us all.

  A. which   B. that   C. who   D. whose

( ) 11. Which of the books _____ were borrowed from him is the best?

  A. which   B. what   C. that   D. whose

( ) 12. Do you know who lives in the building _____ there is a well?

  A. in front of it   B. in front of whose

  C. in front of which   D. in front which

( ) 13. I'll never forget the day _____ I joined the league.

  A. on which   B. in which   C. which   D. at which

( ) 14. The woman _____ my brother spoke just now is my teacher.

  A. who   B. to whom   C. to who   D. whom

( ) 15. Jeanne was her old friend, _____ she borrowed a necklace.

  A. from who   B. from whom   C. to that   D. to whom

( ) 16. His glasses, _____ he was like a blind man, fell to the ground and broke its leg.

  A. which   B. with which   C. without which   D. that

( ) 17. She is a teacher of much knowledge, _____ much can be learned.

A. who B. that C. from which D. from whom

( )18. He built a telescope _____ he could study the skies.

A. in which B. with that C. through which D. by it

( )19. Do you know the reason _____ he was late?

A. that B. which C. for what D. for which

( )20. I have bought two pens, _____ writes well.

A. none of which B. neither of which
C. none of them D. neither of them

( )21. _____ was natural, he married Jenny.

A. Which B. That C. This D. As

( )22. Such signs _____ we use in the experiment _____ Greek letters.

A. as, are B. as, is C. that, are D. that, is

( )23. I passed him a large glass of whisky, _____ he drank immediately.

A. that B. as C. which D. who

( )24. She is very good at dance, _____ everybody knows.

A. that B. which C. who D. as

( )25. It was raining, _____ was a pity.

A. what B. that C. the which D. which

( )26. _____ has been said above, grammar is a set of dead rules.

A. Which B. What C. That D. As

( )27. Is this factory _____ you visited last year?

A. that B. where C. in which D. the one

( )28. Mr Smith is the only one of those foreigners who _____ working in China.

A. is B. has C. have D. are

( )29. Is this the kite _____ you flew yesterday.

A. the one B. which C. that D. the one which

( )30. The reason _____ he made up was obviously false.

A. which B. why C. for which D. on which

二、找出下列句子中错误的选项，并改正过来

1. I want to <u>make friends</u> <u>with</u> the girl <u>who</u> English is pretty <u>good</u>.
     A   B   C   D

Unit 6 Living History of Culture

2. This <u>is</u> the person <u>who</u> you <u>are</u> <u>looking for</u>.
     A   B   C   D

3. He <u>was</u> <u>the first</u> people <u>who</u> <u>passed</u> the exam.
    A   B   C   D

4. <u>Who</u> is <u>the girl</u> <u>who</u> <u>is</u> crying?
    A   B   C D

5. The house, <u>that</u> we <u>bought</u> last month, <u>is</u> very <u>nice</u>.
           A   B   C   D

6. I <u>will</u> never <u>forget</u> the day <u>which</u> I <u>met</u> Mr. Li.
   A   B   C   D

7. The man <u>whom</u> is <u>speaking</u> at <u>the meeting</u> <u>is</u> a farmer.
        A   B   C   D

8. I don't know <u>if</u> he <u>will come</u> home <u>for</u> <u>the</u> festival or not.
            A   B   C D

9. We <u>are talking</u> about <u>if</u> <u>we'll</u> go on <u>the</u> picnic.
      A   B C   D

10. The teacher <u>told</u> us the earth <u>turned</u> <u>around</u> <u>the</u> sun
            A   B   C   D

1.(　　)应为_____　　2.(　　)应为_____　　3.(　　)应为_____

4.(　　)应为_____　　5.(　　)应为_____　　6.(　　)应为_____

7.(　　)应为_____　　8.(　　)应为_____　　9.(　　)应为_____

10.(　　)应为_____

For Better Performance

一、找出与所给单词画线部分读音相同的选项

(　　)1. br<u>a</u>nch   A. br<u>o</u>chure   B. m<u>a</u>chine   C. ch<u>o</u>ose   D. ch<u>e</u>mistry

(　　)2. tr<u>a</u>vel   A. ch<u>a</u>nnel   B. <u>a</u>bility   C. loc<u>a</u>te   D. <u>a</u>cross

(　　)3. <u>o</u>riginally   A. l<u>o</u>nely   B. d<u>o</u>ctor   C. c<u>o</u>st   D. pr<u>o</u>tect

(　　)4. pr<u>e</u>tty   A. m<u>e</u>ntion   B. r<u>e</u>member   C. <u>e</u>mperor   D. s<u>e</u>cret

(　　)5. br<u>i</u>lliant   A. p<u>i</u>t   B. kn<u>i</u>fe   C. s<u>i</u>gn   D. gu<u>i</u>de

二、英汉互译

1. compare with… _____　　2. be interested in… _____

3. in his thirties _____　　4. hearty dishes _____

5. remind sb of _____   6. be made of... _____

7. 走进 _____   8. 全世界 _____

9. 饮食习惯 _____   10. 被列入 _____

11. 以……开始 _____   12. 由于 _____

三、用单词的适当形式填空

1. _____ （culture） exchanges are a way of building bridges between countries.

2. What _____ （exact） is the influence of television on children?

3. We should water the plant _____ （regular）, never letting the soil dry out.

4. There are over 70 pyramids in Egypt, _____ （stretch） down the Nile River Valley.

5. He tries hard to _____ （attractive） to customers.

6. It is better to _____ （伸展） the tight muscles first.

7. The beauty of life only and no and out of the _____ （辉煌的）.

8. This film is very _____ （有吸引力的） to us.

9. There are many _____ （不同） in eating habits among different countries.

10. The wall is made of _____ （石块）.

四、找出下列句子中错误的选项，并改正过来

1. It's the place where I have visited three times.
　　　A　　　B　　C　　　D

2. Every sentence should start in a capital letter.
　　　　A　　　　B　　C　　　　D

3. This is the farm which we worked when we were young.
　　　　　A　　B　　　C　　　　D

4. The reason why he didn't come is because he never got the notice.
　　　　A　　　B　　　　　C　　　　　　D

5. Rice is so an important part of the Asian food culture.
　　　A B　　C　　　　　　　　D

1.（　）应为_____　2.（　）应为_____　3.（　）应为_____

4.（　）应为_____　5.（　）应为_____

Unit 6 Living History of Culture

单元检测

第一部分　英语知识运用(共分三节,满分 40 分)

第一节　语音知识：从 A、B、C、D 四个选项中找出其画线部分与所给单词画线部分读音相同的选项。(共 5 分,每小题 1 分)

(　　)1. p<u>o</u>sition　　A. <u>o</u>pinion　　B. h<u>o</u>nor　　C. an<u>o</u>ther　　D. bl<u>o</u>ck

(　　)2. <u>ex</u>port　　A. <u>ex</u>actly　　B. <u>ex</u>pert　　C. <u>ex</u>perience　　D. <u>ex</u>cuse

(　　)3. <u>a</u>ctive　　A. <u>a</u>pply　　B. <u>a</u>lthough　　C. <u>a</u>pple　　D. <u>a</u>gency

(　　)4. <u>c</u>laim　　A. <u>c</u>rowd　　B. practi<u>c</u>e　　C. adv<u>c</u>e　　D. differen<u>c</u>e

(　　)5. l<u>i</u>fe　　A. <u>i</u>dea　　B. publ<u>i</u>c　　C. c<u>i</u>ty　　D. hol<u>i</u>day

第二节　词汇与语法知识：从 A、B、C、D 四个选项中选出可以填入空白处的最佳选项。(共 25 分,每小题 1 分)

(　　)6. It's the best place _____ I've visited twice.

　　A. which　　B. where　　C. in which　　D. that

(　　)7. Why are you so interested _____ this city?

　　A. in　　B. on　　C. to　　D. of

(　　)8. The warriors are all life-sized and set in _____ rows.

　　A. regular　　B. regularly　　C. good　　D. right

(　　)9. There are over 70 pyramids in Egypt, _____ down the Nile River Valley.

　　A. stretching　　B. stretched　　C. extend　　D. extended

(　　)10. Just as every has a _____ culture, so do their _____ habits.

　　A. differ; eating　　　　B. different; eating

　　C. different; eaten　　　D. difference; eating

(　　)11. One American habit is _____ your food in small pieces upfront and then eating your entire dinner with just a fork.

　　A. cutting up　　　　B. having cutting

　　C. cutting down　　　D. cutting off

(　　)12. Do you know the man _____ your father is talking with?

　　A. whose　　B. what　　C. whom　　D. which

(　　)13. Happiness often comes to those _____ work hard.
　　　　A. what　　　B. which　　　C. whom　　　D. who

(　　)14. It is the village _____ we worked with them.
　　　　A. where　　　B. which　　　C. that　　　D. /

(　　)15. Is there _____ you want to buy in this shop?
　　　　A. something that　　　　　　B. anything that
　　　　C. something which　　　　　 D. anything which

(　　)16. He bought a house, _____ is located in the center of the city.
　　　　A. that　　　B. which　　　C. where　　　D. /

(　　)17. It is fun _____ to tell stories in the dark in the forest.
　　　　A. take turns　　B. in return　　C. taking turns　　D. took turns

(　　)18. Have you known the woman _____ wallet was lost?
　　　　A. which　　　B. whose　　　C. that　　　D. of which

(　　)19. Mary _____ be in the hospital. I saw her play basketball a minute ago.
　　　　A. mustn't　　B. shouldn't　　C. can't　　　D. may not

(　　)20. _____ you succeed in passing the college entrance examination.
　　　　A. Must　　　B. Will　　　C. May　　　D. Can

(　　)21. Beijing Opera is popular _____ old people.
　　　　A. with　　　B. in　　　C. at　　　D. during

(　　)22. If you go there by _____ plane, you'll have _____ comfortable journey.
　　　　A. a;an　　　B. an;a　　　C. the;a　　　D. /;a

(　　)23. The young lady prefers _____ to _____ a car for work.
　　　　A. walk;drive　　　　　　B. to walk;drive
　　　　C. walking;driving　　　　D. to walking;drive

(　　)24. We always have _____ rice for _____ lunch.
　　　　A. /;/　　　B. the;/　　　C. /;a　　　D. the;the

(　　)25. How is everything going with you? _____
　　　　A. Quite well, thank you.　　　B. Good, and you?
　　　　C. No, just so-so.　　　　　　 D. Good, why not?

(　　)26. Susan is becoming _____ in this topic.
　　　　A. much interested　　　　　 B. much interesting
　　　　C. more and more interested　 D. much and much interested

( )27. Handan is _____ that we can hardly visit all the places of interest in two or three days.

  A. so an ancient city   B. such ancient a city
  C. a such ancient city   D. so ancient a city

( )28. —How long are you staying in Guangzhou?
  —_____.

  A. You are welcome   B. It depends
  C. Thank you very much   D. See you later

( )29. It was at the school gate _____ I met an old friend of mine.
  A. that   B. which   C. where   D. why

( )30. The little boy was praised by his father this evening. He _____ well in his study.
  A. should have done to   B. may have done
  C. can have done   D. must have done

第三节　完形填空：阅读下面的短文，从所给的 A、B、C、D 四个选项中选出正确的答案。(共 10 分，每小题 1 分)

Allan was worried. This was his first time to go travelling __31__. He didn't know how __32__ his seat, so he went to the air hostess and asked, "Could you help me? I can't find my seat." The air hostess showed __33__ the seat and told him __34__ and fasten the seat belt(系好安全带). She told Allan __35__ about when the plane was going __36__. And she also said that Allan's ears might feel a little strange, but he didn't need to __37__ it because many people felt like that. When the plane was flying very __38__, Allan could stand up and walk around. He could also read books, newspapers or see films. The air hostess would __39__ food and drinks. Allan would enjoy the flight and __40__ soon.

( )31. A. by ship   B. by air   C. by car   D. by bus
( )32. A. find   B. finding   C. to find   D. to found
( )33. A. him   B. me   C. her   D. he
( )34. A. stand up   B. sleep   C. to sit down   D. sit down
( )35. A. didn't move   B. to not move   C. not to move   D. not move
( )36. A. down   B. up   C. over   D. through
( )37. A. worrying   B. be worried   C. worry about   D. worry
( )38. A. high   B. slow   C. quiet   D. highly

(　　)39. A. hold B. take C. bring D. carry

(　　)40. A. arrive home B. arrive to home C. get to home D. reach to home

第二部分　篇章与词汇理解(共分三节　满分 50 分)

第一节　阅读理解：阅读下列短文，从每题所给的 A、B、C、D 四个选项中，选出最恰当的答案。(共 30 分，每小题 2 分)

A

The Great Wall of China is called the "Ten thousand Li Great Wall" in Chinese. In fact, it's more than 6,000 kilometers long. It winds its way from west to east, across deserts, over mountains, through valleys till at last it reaches the sea. It is one of the wonders of the world.

The Great Wall has a history of over twenty centuries. The first part of it was built during the Spring and Autumn Period. During the Warring States Period, more walls were put up to defend the borders of different kingdoms. It was during the Qin Dynasty that the kingdom of Qin united the different parts into one empire. To keep the enemy out of his empire, Emperor Qin Shihuang had all the walls joined up. Thus, the Great Wall came into being.

The Great Wall is wide enough at the top for five horses or ten men to walk side by side. Along the wall are watchtowers, where soldiers used to keep watch. Fires were lit on the towers as a warning when the enemy came.

It was very difficult to build such a wall in the ancient days without any modern machines. All the work was done by hand. Thousands of men died and were buried under the wall they built. The Great Wall was made not only of stone and earth, but of the flesh and blood of millions of men.

Today the Great Wall has become a place of interest not only to the Chinese but to people from all over the world. Many of them have come to know the famous Chinese saying: "He who does not reach the Great Wall is not a true man."

(　　)41. Which of the following is NOT true?

A. The Great Wall is called the "Ten thousand Li Great Wall" in Chinese.

B. The Great Wall is less than 6,000 kilometers long.

C. The Great Wall winds its way from west to east and reaches the sea at last.

D. The Great Wall is one of the wonders of the world.

(　　)42. People started to build the Great Wall in _____.

A. the Spring and Autumn Period B. the Warring States Period

Unit 6　Living History of Culture

C. the Qin Dynasty　　　　D. New China

(　　)43. _____ joined up all the walls.

A. The enemy　　　　B. Emperor Qin Shihuang

C. Modern machines　　　　D. People from all over the world

(　　)44. What is the underlined words "side by side" mean in Chinese?

A. 肩并肩　　B. 一边一边地　　C. 两侧　　D. 通过

(　　)45. What is the best title of the passage?

A. The History of the Great Wall　　B. Welcome to the Great Wall

C. The Great Wall　　　　D. The Famous Chinese Saying

B

If you stay in an Indian home, bring something from your home country as a gift. Although it is not expected, it would be much pleasant. But find out the social position and religion of your hosts before you choose the gift. A bottle of foreign whisky would be the perfect gift for some, but not at all suitable for others. If you know the people you are going to stay with, it is a good idea to ask them what they would like. Some things are just not available in India.

It is not necessary to bring a gift when you are invited to dinner. After all, you are the honored guest. Several years ago, it was almost unpleasant to bring sweets or a bottle of wine. But this is not true today. Nowadays it is a custom which is becoming popular with many Indians. Fruit, flowers or a box of sweets are perfect gifts, and will make no one unhappy.

In all classes of society, both in the city and in the country, food is only taken to the mouth with the right hand. This is the most important part of the etiquette(礼节) of eating in India. When you watch Indians eat something, you will see that they keep their left. hands on their legs.

If you want to find a conversation topic in India, talk about families. Another useful subject to start with is cricket(板球). But once you get to know a person better, any topic is acceptable. Indians love to talk about politics and religion. They enjoy heated discussions. Conversation is an art form and people take the time to really talk.

(　　)46. While visiting an Indian home, your hosts will be _____ to get a gift from your country.

A. happy　　B. angry　　C. worried　　D. sad

(　　)47. If you are invited for a meal at an Indian home, _____.

A. you should pay for the food

— 105 —

B. you will hurt your hosts if you take anything

C. it is fashionable to take flowers or sweets

D. it is traditional to take whisky

( )48. Indians love interesting topics and they _____.

A. only talk about family matters

B. prefer to have heated discussions

C. don't like talking about themselves

D. get away from religion and politics

( )49. The underlined part in the first paragraph means _____.

A. you can buy these things easily in India

B. they don't make these things in India

C. they never avoid these things in India

D. you can't get these things in India

( )50. According to the passage, all of the following are true EXCEPT that _____.

A. your choice of gift will depend on who your hosts are

B. playing cricket with left hand is popular in India

C. Indians normally use their right hands for food they eat

D. Indians like to talk about serious things with guests

C

Beijing Opera, also called Peking Opera, is our national opera. It came into being(形成) after 1790 and has a history of over 200 years. Its music and singing came from Xipi and Erhuang in Anhui and Hubei. The Guangxu Emperor(帝王) and Empress Dowager Cixi were also crazy about Beijing Opera and helped develop the art form.

There are four main roles in Beijing Opera: Sheng, Dan, Jing, Chou. Sheng is the leading male(男性) actor. For example, a Wusheng is a soldier or fighter. A Xiaosheng is a young man. A Laosheng is an old man with beard(胡子). Dan is the female(女性) role. Jing, mostly male, is the face painted role and Chou is the comedy(喜剧) actor or clown(小丑).

Beijing Opera is full of famous stories, beautiful facial paintings, wonderful gestures and fighting. Some of the stories are from history books, but most are from famous novels. The people in the stories usually can't agree with each other. They become angry, unhappy, sad and lonely. Sometimes they are afraid and worried. Then they find a way to make peace with(与……讲和)

each other. Everyone is usually happy in the end.

Beijing Opera is an important part of Chinese culture. In China, it used to be popular with old people while young people didn't like it very much. However, more young people are becoming interested in it nowadays. And more people around the world are learning about Beijing Opera's special singing, acting and facial paintings.

(   )51. Beijing Opera's singing is from _____.

   A. Anhui and Hubei   B. Beijing and Anhui

   C. the history book   D. the literature and novels

(   )52. The second paragraph of the passage is about the _____ of Beijing Opera.

   A. stories B. roles C. gestures D. paintings

(   )53. From the passage, we know the role Chou most probably has a(n) _____ feature.

   A. honest B. funny C. boring D. serious

(   )54. You can most probably read this kind of passage _____.

   A. in a geography textbook   B. in a science and technology magazine

   C. in a business report   D. on a culture website

(   )55. Which is TRUE according to the passage?

   A. Peking Opera is full of different gestures.

   B. There are only four roles in Beijing Opera.

   C. Beijing Opera is the most popular in the world.

   D. The people in the story usually are in agreement.

第二节　词义搭配：从(B)栏中选出(A)栏单词的正确解释。(共10分,每小题1分)

    A   B

(   )56. attract   A. having power to arouse interest

(   )57. destination B. different from others

(   )58. discover   C. the place where you want to go

(   )59. distance   D. on behalf of; stand for

(   )60. forecast   E. making a strong impression

(   )61. impressive F. long before

(   )62. represent   G. a feeling of surprise

(   )63. unique   H. a prediction about how something will develop

(   )64. wonder   I. find; observe

(　　)65. ancient　　　　J. the length between two places

第三节　补全对话：根据对话内容，从对话后的选项中选出能填入空白处的最佳选项。(共 10 分，每小题 2 分)

A：Hi! Bob. Come in, please.

B：Hi!　66　

A：I'm looking for information about Hainan on the Internet. I'm going to Hainan for my holiday　67　

B：No, but my father has been there twice. He told me there were many interesting places.　68　

A：I'm leaving at 9 a. m. on Friday, July.

B：　69　

A：I will go there by train.

B：Have you ever flown in a plane?

A：　70　

B：You must be excited when you fly in a plane.

A：Really? I can't wait for it.

> A. Have you ever been to Hainan?
> B. How will you go there?
> C. No, never.
> D. What are you doing now?
> E. When are you leaving?

第三部分　语言技能运用(共分四节　满分 30 分)

第一节　单词拼写：根据下列句子及所给汉语注释，在横线上写出该单词。(共 5 分，每小题 1 分)

71. This is a _____ (典型的) example of Roman pottery.

72. Everyone comes back home for _____ (庆祝).

73. It is one of the most _____ (令人震惊的) films I've ever seen.

74. The headmaster made a bad _____ (印象) on the parents.

75. Do you know something _____ (历史) of Chinese arts.

Unit 6 Living History of Culture

第二节 词形变换：用括号内单词的适当形式填空，将正确答案写在横线上。（共 5 分，每小题 1 分）

76. There is an _____ (introduce) to Mount Tai on the wall.

77. How _____ (wonder) if I know English and French both!

78. The Spring Festival is a _____ (tradition) festival.

79. _____ (attract) by the beauty of nature, the girl decided to spend another two days on the farm.

80. I never forget our hometown's _____ (beautiful).

第三节 改错：从 A、B、C、D 四个画线处找出一处错误的选项，并写出正确答案。（共 10 分，每小题 2 分）

81. There <u>are</u> so <u>many</u> <u>pleasure</u> in <u>our life</u>.
       A   B   C   D

82. Peking Opera is listed <u>as</u> <u>one of</u> the <u>cultural</u> <u>treasure</u> of China.
                    A   B   C   D

83. He is <u>only</u> one of the <u>teachers</u> <u>who</u> <u>own</u> a lot of knowledge.
      A   B   C D

84. What <u>were</u> you <u>do</u> <u>when</u> the teacher <u>came</u> in?
       A   B C   D

85. I <u>want</u> to <u>learn</u> <u>from</u> Chinese <u>history</u>.
   A   B   C   D

81. (　　)应为 _____　　82. (　　)应为 _____　　83. (　　)应为 _____

84. (　　)应为 _____　　85. (　　)应为 _____

第四节 书面表达（共 10 分）

作文题目：Paper Cutting。

词数要求：80~100 词。

写作要点：介绍中国的剪纸文化。（简单介绍中国剪纸文化的历史、特点以及自己对剪纸文化的看法）

_____

_____

_____

_____

Unit 7

Natural Disasters

Warming-up

一、句型汇总

1. My flight/train… is canceled/delayed due to the typhoon/floods. 我的航班/火车……由于台风/洪水……被取消/推迟。

2. Some of the natural disasters are caused by human activities. 一些自然灾害是人类活动产生的。

3. It seems there have been more floods/typhoon… than before. 比起从前,现在似乎有更多的洪水/台风……发生。

4. Promoting the use of green energy. 推广绿色能源的使用。

5. People are advised to use electric cars and public transportation. 人们被建议使用电车和公共交通。

6. Private cars powered by petrol lead to air pollution, traffic jam and noise. 以汽油为能源的私家车会导致空气污染、交通堵塞和噪声。

7. Typhoon and floods strike more frequently and with greater force than before. 相较于从前,台风和洪水袭来得更加频繁且威力更大。

二、英汉互译

1. typhoon _____   2. drought _____
3. earthquake _____   4. flood _____
5. heat waves _____   6. sandstorm _____

7. acid rain _____   8. vehicle _____
9. volcano _____   10. urban _____
11. frequently _____   12. force _____
13. discussion _____   14. 保护……以防…… _____
15. 防止_____   16. 可持续发展_____
17. 由于 _____   18. 被……污染 _____
19. 由……引起;导致_____ 20. 损失(n) _____
21. 做出改变 _____   22. 提升,提高,促进 _____
23. 与……联系在一起;使束缚于…… _____

Listening and Speaking

一、找出与所给单词画线部分读音相同的选项

(　　) 1. fl<u>oo</u>d   A. f<u>oo</u>d   B. bl<u>oo</u>d   C. typh<u>oo</u>n   D. m<u>oo</u>d
(　　) 2. d<u>e</u>lay   A. d<u>e</u>light   B. d<u>e</u>sert   C. d<u>e</u>velopment D. b<u>e</u>ar
(　　) 3. cancel<u>ed</u> A. caus<u>ed</u>   B. want<u>ed</u>   C. decid<u>ed</u>   D. stopp<u>ed</u>
(　　) 4. sugges<u>tion</u> A. transporta<u>tion</u> B. ques<u>tion</u> C. na<u>tion</u>   D. promo<u>tion</u>
(　　) 5. pr<u>o</u>tect A. pr<u>o</u>mote   B. pr<u>o</u>bably   C. pr<u>o</u>mise   D. pr<u>o</u>ject

二、从 B 栏中找出与 A 栏中相对应的答语

A

1. What's wrong with you?
2. What should we do to protect the environment?
3. Why do typhoons strike more frequently than before?
4. What kinds of natural disasters do you know?
5. Do you think some of the natural disasters are caused by human?

B

A. We should plant more trees.
B. My flight is delayed due to the floods.
C. Because human activities.
D. Yes, I agree with you.
E. Typhoon, drought, earthquake…and so on.

三、用所给句子补全下面对话

A：I thought you were going to Thailand this morning.

B：__1__

A：That's terrible. It seems there have been more floods than before.

B：__2__

A：Some of them are caused by human activities.

B：__3__

A：Well, it's lucky that people have decided to make a change.

B：__4__

A：__5__

> A. My flight is delayed due to the floods.
> B. Yes. We've burned too much coal and oil.
> C. That's certainly true.
> D. Yes. It is what we should do right now.
> E. I agree with you.

四、场景模拟

编写一组对话。因为台风导致 Chen Jie 飞往泰国的航班被迫取消，好友 Mary Fisher 询问情况，两人就人类活动对自然灾害产生的影响进行讨论。

提示词汇：human activities/Thailand/It seems there have been more… than before

Reading and Writing

一、用单词的适当形式填空

1. We should promote the use of green _____（能源，能量）.

2. Sixty-seven percent _____（城市）people use the Internet.

3. Humans are _____（有责任的）for many natural disasters.

4. Sandstorms, acid rain and smog happen more _____（频繁地）than before.

5. There are more and more _____（讨论）on natural disasters in recent years.

6. Sandstorms are _____（cause）naturally by strong winds.

Unit 7 Natural Disasters

7. Many of the natural disasters are due to _____ (environment) damages.

8. It is lucky that humans have realized the _____ (important) of sustainable development.

9. It is known that sandstorms are caused _____ (nature) by strong winds.

10. _____ (promote) the use of green energy is useful.

二、完形填空

The sky was clear and the sun was shining brightly before the deadly disaster of the typhoon. Bernadette Tenegra, a 44-year-old high school teacher, was in her __1__ which was on the bank of a river. The Tenegra family stayed together in their shelter to keep away from the storm. They thought that the powerful storm would die out soon as it did __2__. So they were just hanging on there.

But things didn't happen __3__ they had thought. The water rose with a frightening speed and their __4__ house fell down, sweeping away the occupants(居住者), including Tenegra's husband and her other daughters. They were able to struggle to __5__, but the 6-year-old Tenegra was __6__ against the strong wind and water, along with sharp deadly debris (残骸). Bernadette made her way to the child and was holding her and kept __7__ her to keep on.

"I crawled(爬) over to her, and I tried to pull her up. But she was too __8__ and wasn't able to make it. It seemed she had already __9__," Tenegra said, crying. "I screamed but it didn't work."

The mother said __10__ that she would never forget the last words of her daughter before death, "Mom, just let go, just let go. Save yourself. I love you forever."

(　　)1. A. family   B. school   C. building   D. home
(　　)2. A. in the past   B. in the day   C. in the end   D. in the future
(　　)3. A. while   B. before   C. as   D. since
(　　)4. A. wooden   B. golden   C. hidden   D. modern
(　　)5. A. strength   B. warmth   C. safety   D. difficulty
(　　)6. A. fighting   B. beating   C. touching   D. preventing
(　　)7. A. inviting   B. ordering   C. training   D. telling
(　　)8. A. sleepy   B. weak   C. impatient   D. careless
(　　)9. A. given back   B. given away   C. given up   D. given off
(　　)10. A. excitedly   B. sadly   C. angrily   D. confidently

三、阅读理解

阅读下面短文,从每题所给的 A、B、C、D 四个选项中选出最佳答案。

— 113 —

At present, too much carbon dioxide(二氧化碳) makes the earth warmer and warmer and causes terrible effect to human beings. To save our plant, to save ourselves, a new lifestyle called low-carbon life(低碳生活) becomes popular. Low carbon means low energy and no waste. It is necessary for everybody to learn to live a low-carbon life.

To live a low-carbon life, we'd better save energy as much as possible. Turn off the lights and TV whenever they are not needed. If possible, use cold water to wash clothes or dishes. Take a short shower and try to take a cold one when the weather gets warm. Don't do the cooking with electricity.

To live a low-carbon life we should eat less meat. Everybody knows eating too much meat makes people fat and easy to have heart disease, but maybe you don't know keeping animals for food produces even more carbon dioxide than all the cars in the world, and being a vegetarian can help reduce(减少) one and a half tons(吨) of carbon dioxide a year. Maybe it is a little difficult, but it's really necessary.

To live a low-carbon life, we are supposed to do less shopping. When we go shopping we may drive a car or take other transportation. On the one hand, these machines pollute the air and waste energy. On the other hand, most of us always buy some useless things because of some advertisements. It is not only a waste of money but also causes trouble to the earth, because as you know, making everything will produce carbon dioxide more or less.

There are many other ways to live a low-carbon life, such as recycling things, planting trees and reusing textbooks. If we can keep it a habit in our daily life, the earth will become a safer planet for us to live on.

(　　)1. _____ makes the weather on the earth get warmer.

　　A. Little rubbish　　　　　　B. A waste of money

　　C. Too much carbon dioxide　　D. People's breath

(　　)2. We can _____ to save energy in our daily life.

　　A. use less electricity　　　　B. go to sleep with lights on

　　C. wash clothes with hot water　D. waste water

(　　)3. The underlined word "it" in the third paragraph means _____.

　　A. eating less meat　　　　　B. having heart diseases

　　C. keeping animals for food　　D. eating less vegetables

(　　)4. Less shopping should be done because _____.

　　A. wasting money causes trouble to people

　　B. the advertisements are sometimes misleading

　　C. the less you shop, the less carbon dioxide will be produced

D. we have nothing to buy

( )5. If everybody lives a low-carbon life, _____.

    A. we will waste more energy

    B. there will be less carbon dioxide

    C. the earth will become a dangerous place to live on

    D. we will feel unhappy

四、书面表达

以"Improve the environment"为题,写一篇文章,字数80~100字。

_____
_____
_____
_____

Grammar

一、从下面每小题四个选项中选出最佳选项

( )1. _____ we are doing has never been done before.

    A. That   B. What   C. Which   D. Whether

( )2. _____ she was invited to the ball made her very happy.

    A. What   B. That   C. When   D. Because

( )3. _____ do you think will teach us maths next term?

    A. Whom   B. Who   C. What   D. That

( )4. _____ you did it is not known to all.

    A. Who   B. What   C. How   D. Which

( )5. _____ you do should be well done.

    A. How   B. That   C. Whatever   D. Why

( )6. _____ we'll go camping tomorrow depends on the weather.

    A. If   B. Whether   C. That   D. Where

( )7. _____ was said here must be kept secret.

    A. Who   B. The thing   C. Whatever   D. Where

( )8. It's a great pity _____ we won't be able to finish the task on time.
   A. when B. that C. why D. where

( )9. _____ that there is another good harvest this year.
   A. It says B. It is said C. It was said D. He was said

( )10. _____ appeared to me that he enjoyed the food very much.
   A. What B. It C. All that D. That

( )11. It is very clear _____ our policy is a correct one.
   A. what B. that C. why D. where

( )12. _____ is most important to me is that I don't have to go to work by ferry.
   A. What B. That C. It D. There

( )13. It has not been decided _____ they will leave for New York.
   A. when B. why C. that D. what

( )14. _____ goes against nature will be punished.
   A. No matter who   B. Who
   C. Whoever   D. Anybody

( )15. It has been proved _____ eating vegetables in childhood helps to protect you against serious illnesses in later life.
   A. if B. because C. when D. that

( )16. Obviously _____ we do morning exercises every day _____ us good.
   A. that; do B. if; do C. what; does D. that; does

( )17. _____ is still a question _____ will win.
   A. It; that B. It; who C. That; who D. This; that

( )18. _____ has passed the test will get a prize.
   A. Whoever B. No mater who C. Whomever D. Who

( )19. Is _____ true that the famous scientist will give us a lecture next week?
   A. that B. it C. his D. he

( )20. _____ is no possibility _____ Bob can win the first prize in the match.
   A. There; that B. It; that C. there; whether D. It; whether

( )21. —Tom failed in the exam again.
   —That is _____ he didn't follow the teacher's advice.
   A. why B. how C. for D. because

( )22. The reason I have to go is _____ if I don't.
   A. that she will be disappointed
   B. because she will be disappointed

C. on account of her being disappointed

D. that she will be disappointing

(　　) 23. She looked _____ she were ten years younger.
   A. that B. like C. as D. as though

(　　) 24. The reason I plan to go is _____ she will be disappointed if I don't.
   A. because B. that C. thanks to D. what

(　　) 25. _____ made the school proud was _____ more than 90% of the students had been admitted to key universities.
   A. What; because B. What; that
   C. That; what D. That; because

(　　) 26. It is said _____ _____ was all _____ he said.
   A. that; that; that B. what; what; what
   C. that; which; what D. that; that; which

(　　) 27. _____ moved us most was _____ he looked after the old man for more than twenty years.
   A. That; that B. What; that C. What; what D. That; what

(　　) 28. _____ he does has nothing to do with me.
   A. Whatever B. No matter what C. That D. If

(　　) 29. Is _____ he said really true?
   A. that B. what C. why D. whether

(　　) 30. _____ the meeting should last two days or three days doesn't matter.
   A. That B. Whether C. If D. Where

二、找出下列句子中错误的选项，并改正过来

1. There is believed that greenhouse gases are the main causes of global warming.
  A   B   C   D

2. If he can finish his task on time is of great importance.
 A   B   C D

3. The problem is whom will take charge of our class.
     A B C D

4. It is likely which he will make great progress in his study.
 A   B   C D

5. It is report that no one passes the exam.
 A B C D

6. My suggestion is that we will start early tomorrow.
    A B C   D

7. That is impossible for the 3- year-old boy to go shopping by himself.
   　A　　　　　　　　　　　　B　　　　　　　　C　　　　D
8. Where did they hold the important meeting yesterday is unknown to us.
   　　　　A　　　　　　　　　　　　　　　　　　　B　　C　　　　D
9. That the sports meeting will be held is decided by our team leader.
   　A　　　　　　　　　B　　　　C　　　D
10. Tom is no longer who he used to be.
    　　　　A　　　B　　C　　D

1.(　　)应为_____　2.(　　)应为_____　3.(　　)应为_____
4.(　　)应为_____　5.(　　)应为_____　6.(　　)应为_____
7.(　　)应为_____　8.(　　)应为_____　9.(　　)应为_____
10.(　　)应为_____

For Better Performance

一、找出与所给单词画线部分读音相同的选项

(　　)1. prot<u>e</u>ct　　A. pr<u>e</u>vent　　B. v<u>e</u>hicle　　C. d<u>e</u>finitely　　D. <u>e</u>lectric

(　　)2. <u>h</u>eat　　A. <u>h</u>onest　　B. <u>h</u>our　　C. <u>h</u>onor　　D. <u>h</u>old

(　　)3. typh<u>oo</u>n　　A. fl<u>oo</u>d　　B. b<u>oo</u>k　　C. w<u>oo</u>d　　D. f<u>oo</u>l

(　　)4. s<u>u</u>stainable　　A. <u>au</u>tumn　　B. red<u>u</u>ce　　C. b<u>u</u>s　　D. r<u>u</u>ler

(　　)5. w<u>a</u>ve　　A. <u>a</u>shamed　　B. he<u>a</u>dache　　C. ex<u>a</u>m　　D. <u>a</u>ction

二、英汉互译

1. lead to _____　　2. due to _____

3. more and more _____　　4. It is known that… _____

5. sustainable development _____　　6. be responsible for… _____

7. 交通堵塞 _____　　8. 私家车 _____

9. 自然灾害 _____　　10. 做某事是…… _____

11. 电车 _____

三、用单词的适当形式填空

1. Our environment is badly _____ (pollute) by human activities.

2. Private cars _____ (power) by petrol lead to air pollution.

3. A _____ (grow) number of countries have set targets for electric vehicle sales.

Unit 7 Natural Disasters

4. Today, _____ (nature) disasters strike more frequently than before.

5. It's time for us _____ (make) a change.

6. Scientists believe that natural disasters are caused by human _____ (活动).

7. Sandstorms happen more _____ (频繁) than before.

8. People are advised to use _____ (公共的,公众的) transportation.

9. My flight is _____ (取消) due to the typhoon.

10. It seems there have been more _____ (洪水) these years than before.

四、找出下列句子中错误的选项,并改正过来

1. Humans are responsible to natural disasters.
   　A　　　　B　　　　C　　D

2. Sandstorms happen frequently than before.
   　　　　　A　　　B　　　　C　　D

3. It is known that sandstorms cause naturally by strong winds.
   　A　　B　　　C　　　　　　　D

4. Some people do not pay enough attention smog.
   　　　　　　　A　　　B　　　C　　　　　D

5. We should make some change to the environment.
   　　　　　　A　　　B　　　C　　D

1.(　) 应为_____   2.(　) 应为_____   3.(　) 应为_____
4.(　) 应为_____   5.(　) 应为_____

单元检测

第一部分　英语知识运用(共分三节,满分40分)

第一节　语音知识：从 A、B、C、D 四个选项中找出其画线部分与所给单词画线部分读音相同的选项。(共5分,每小题1分)

(　)1. global   A. whole   B. smog   C. develop   D. follow

(　)2. expert   A. extract   B. example   C. excuse   D. exact

(　)3. rapid   A. possible   B. acid   C. realize   D. flight

(　)4. reduce   A. regular   B. repeat   C. relative   D. rest

(　)5. tie   A. friend   B. believe   C. lie   D. relief

第二节　词汇与语法知识： 从 A、B、C、D 四个选项中选出可以填入空白处的最佳选项。(共 25 分，每小题 1 分)

(　　) 6. My flight is canceled _____ the typhoon.
　　　　A. due to　　　　B. due for　　　　C. due　　　　D. /

(　　) 7. We have burned _____ coal and oil and badly polluted the environment.
　　　　A. too much　　　B. much too　　　C. too many　　D. many

(　　) 8. The most important thing is _____.
　　　　A. how we can pass the exam　　　B. how can we pass the exam
　　　　C. how do we can pass the exam　　D. how we could pass the exam

(　　) 9. I will not agree _____ support your plan _____ you show me your sincerity.
　　　　A. with; if　　B. to; once　　C. for; unless　　D. to; unless

(　　) 10. If more people work together, it _____ possible for us to protect our earth.
　　　　A. will be　　B. is　　C. will is　　D. /

(　　) 11. We should _____ our students _____ being hurt by bad people.
　　　　A. protect; from
　　　　B. protect; against
　　　　C. provide; for
　　　　D. A and B

(　　) 12. Humans are responsible _____ many natural disasters.
　　　　A. for　　B. to　　C. about　　D. of

(　　) 13. Experts _____ the pollution _____ the rapid urban development.
　　　　A. tie; to　　B. tie; for　　C. tie; /　　D. tie; with

(　　) 14. Is _____ necessary for us to look for the old factory after so many years?
　　　　A. this　　B. that　　C. it　　D. there

(　　) 15. It is well _____ the earth runs around the sun.
　　　　A. knew that　　B. known　　C. known that　　D. knew

(　　) 16. People around are forced _____ in the smoke when a person smokes.
　　　　A. to breathe　　B. to be breathe　　C. breathe　　D. breathing

(　　) 17. Tom as well as his parents _____ very kind.
　　　　A. are　　B. is　　C. was　　D. were

(　　) 18. Natural disasters happen _____ than before.
　　　　A. frequent　　B. frequently　　C. more frequently　　D. more frequent

(　　) 19. We should be _____ the environment.
　　　　A. concerned about
　　　　B. concern about
　　　　C. concern
　　　　D. concerned for

(　　) 20. _____ people choose electric cars because they are cheaper than petrol cars.

A. More and more　　　　　B. Less and less
C. Many and many　　　　　D. More and less

(　)21. _____ we will attend the meeting or not is not decided.
A. If　　　B. That　　　C. Whether　　　D. When

(　)22. There is no doubt _____ we will beat their football team.
A. that　　　B. whether　　　C. if　　　D. where

(　)23. The house is _____ I was born and grew up.
A. what　　　B. that　　　C. where　　　D. which

(　)24. _____ I can't accept is _____ he never admitted his mistake.
A What; why　B. What; what　C. What; how　D. What; that

(　)25. The reason _____ I have to leave is _____ my father is ill.
A. why; why　B. why; that　C. that; why　D. that; that

(　)26. That is _____ he was late for school yesterday.
A. what　　　B. why　　　C. that　　　D. whether

(　)27. The trouble is _____ we don't have enough food to eat.
A. what　　　B. whether　　　C. that　　　D. if

(　)28. _____ wants to join the club must sign his name here.
A. Whoever　B. Everyone　C. Each　　　D. Anyone

(　)29. I have no idea _____ he used to be ten years ago.
A. who　　　B. whether　　　C. what　　　D. that

(　)30. _____ he knew the secret is so clear to everyone.
A. Who　　　B. Whether　　　C. What　　　D. That

第三节　完形填空：阅读下面的短文，从所给的 A、B、C、D 四个选项中选出正确的答案。(共 10 分，每小题 0.5 分)

Earthquakes are common; thousands of them happen each day. But most are too weak to feel. During a ___31___ earthquake, there is often a great noise first. Then the earth shakes terribly and many houses fall down. Railway tracks break and trains go off lines; a great many factories are ___32___; thousands of deaths are caused, and many more lose homes… ___33___ the great damage and deaths caused by the earthquake ___34___, other disasters such as fires often ___35___. More buildings are destroyed and more ___36___ caused.

It is well known of the dangers of a possible earthquake, and for centuries man has been making researches on earthquakes. More than 2,000 years ago, ___37___, a Chinese scientist named Zhang Heng ___38___ a machine which could find out from which ___39___ the seismic (地震的) waves had come, and this machine is still ___40___ by scientists today.

No one can stop natural earthquakes. However, scientists can help stop earthquakes destroying.

( ) 31. A. real　　　　　B. weak　　　　　C. big　　　　　　D. small
( ) 32. A. burst　　　　　B. struck　　　　　C. destroyed　　　D. buried
( ) 33. A. Except　　　　B. Besides　　　　C. Instead of　　　D. Because of
( ) 34. A. lonely　　　　　B. later　　　　　C. themselves　　　D. itself
( ) 35. A. follow　　　　　B. copy　　　　　C. come　　　　　D. enter
( ) 36. A. quakes　　　　B. deaths　　　　　C. difficulties　　　D. results
( ) 37. A. as a result　　B. in fact　　　　　C. for example　　D. as well
( ) 38. A. invented　　　B. discovered　　　C. found　　　　　D. bought
( ) 39. A. country　　　　B. directions　　　C. ways　　　　　D. city
( ) 40. A. improved　　　B. repaired　　　　C. protected　　　D. used

第二部分　篇章与词汇理解(共分三节　满分50分)

第一节　阅读理解: 阅读下列短文,从每题所给的 A、B、C、D 四个选项中,选出最恰当的答案。(共30分,每小题2分)

A

No Car Day was first started by 34 cities in France on September 22,1998. It was started to protect the environment. By now, more than 1,000 cities around the world have had a No Car Day.

The first No Car Day in China was in Chengdu in 2001. Other cities, including Taipei, Shanghai and Wuhan, also support(支持) the day.

In Beijing, more and more people are joining in the activity. It asks drivers to leave their cars at home for one day each month and walk or ride a bike to work. It also calls on Beijingers not to use cars on June 5(World Environment Day). The slogan(口号) for the day is, "If we drive for one less day, we can have one more nice day."

So far, more than 200,000 drivers have shown their support. "We can't control the weather, but we can choose not to drive," said Wu Zonghua, an ear club chairman. Beijing is trying to have 238 blue sky days this year. In the first quarter of this year, Beijing only had 52 blue sky days. This was 11 days less than the number for the same period last year. Much of the dust(灰尘) comes from the desert(沙漠), but cars cause most of the air pollution(污染). We must do more for No Car Day.

( ) 41. There are _____ cities in China that support No Car Day according to the passage.
　　　A. three　　　　B. four　　　　C. five　　　　D. six

(   )42. The activity of No Car Day encourages Beijing drivers _____.
   A. not to work on No Car Day
   B. to enjoy having a day off
   C. to leave their cars at home for repair
   D. to ride a bike or walk instead of driving to work

(   )43. According to the passage there were _____ blue sky days in the first quarter of last year in Beijing.
   A. 52   B. 63   C. 41   D. 238

(   )44. The air pollution in Beijing is mostly caused by _____.
   A. cars   B. dust   C. weather   D. rubbish

(   )45. We can know from the passage that _____.
   A. more and more people in Beijing are joining car clubs
   B. people will have one more World Environment Day each month
   C. more and more people won't drive on No Car Day in Beijing
   D. more people in the world won't drive any more

B

More and more people like bicycling and it is no surprise. It is fun, healthy and good for the environment. Maybe that's why there are 1.4 billion bicycles and only 400 million cars on roads worldwide today. Bikes can take you almost anywhere, and there is no oil cost!

Get on a bicycle and ride around your neighbourhood. You may discover something new all around you. Stopping and getting off a bike is easier than stopping and getting out of your car. You can bike to work and benefit(受益) from the enjoyable exercise without polluting the environment. You don't even have to ride all the way.

Folding(叠) bikes work well for people who ride the train. Just fold the bike and take it with you. You can do the same on an airplane. A folding bike can be packed in a suitcase. You can also take a common bike with you when you fly. But be sure to look for information by getting on airline websites. Not all airlines are bicycle-friendly to travelers.

Health Benefits of Bicycling:

It helps to prevent heart diseases.

Bicycling helps to control your weight.

A 15-minute bike ride to and from work three times a week burns off five kilos of fat in a year.

Bicycling can improve your mood(心情).

Exercise like bicycling has been shown to make people feel better, more relaxed and self-confident.

Bicycling is healthier than driving.

(　　)46. From the passage, we know that bicycling is becoming very _____.
  A. surprising B. exciting C. expensive D. popular

(　　)47. When you are riding your bicycle around your neighbourhood, you may _____.
  A. pollute the environment around B. find something you didn't notice
  C. go everywhere and use a little oil D. get off your bike and begin to work

(　　)48. If you travel with a folding bike, you can fold it and _____.
  A. get out of the car B. take it onto a train
  C. put it in your purse D. go on airline websites

(　　)49. One of the benefits from bicycling is that _____.
  A. you can fold the bicycle B. you will be friendly to others
  C. you will be more relaxed D. you may get fatter and fatter

(　　)50. Which is TRUE according to the passage?
  A. Bicycling is enjoyable exercise for people.
  B. Driving cars is healthier than riding bikes.
  C. Riding a bike pollutes your neighbourhood.
  D. Common bikes are welcomed by all airlines.

C

The world is not only hungry but also thirsty for water. This may seem strange to you, since nearly 70% of the earth's surface is covered with water. But about 97% of that is sea water or salt water. Man can only drink and use the other 3% of fresh water from rivers, lakes, underground and so on. And we can not even use all of that because some of it has been made dirty.

Earth Day is April 22. But on all other days, we must also remember how important water is. The water that we use is the most important natural resource on the earth. Today we face serious water problems. One of them is water pollution. All kinds of things from cars, factories, farms and homes make our rivers, lakes and oceans dirty. Polluted water is very bad for people to drink. And dirty water is bad for fish, too.

How do cars and factories make our water dirty? First, they pollute the air. Then, when it rains, the rain water makes our drinking water dirty. Dirty rain, called acid rain(酸雨), is also bad for plants, animals and buildings. Scientists say that in 30 years, more than half of the people in the world won't have enough clean water. We have to learn how to stop wasting water. One of the first step is to develop ways of reusing it. Today in most large cities, water is used only once and then sent out into a sewer system(下水道). From there it returns to the sea or goes underground.

But even though every large city reused its water, we would still not have enough. So we should make use of sea water by removing the salt in it. If we can take these steps, fresh water won't be used up.

( )51. The world is thirsty for water because _____.

　　A. we don't have enough fresh water

　　B. a lot of water goes into sewer systems

　　C. only 70% of the earth's surface is water

　　D. sea water is widely used rather than fresh water

( )52. The underlined word "face" means " _____ ".

　　A. turn the face down　　B. turn the face up

　　C. turn the face to　　　D. turn the face back

( )53. From this passage, we know acid rain _____.

　　A. is only bad for living things

　　B. is not bad for buildings and factories

　　C. can be produced in factories

　　D. is bad for people, animals, plants and buildings

( )54. One difficult way we can solve the problem is to _____.

　　A. use the water with salt in it　　B. remove the salt from sea water

　　C. get water from underground　　D. reuse the water in cities

( )55. What is the best title for this passage?

　　A. Fresh water and sea water.　　B. A thirsty country.

　　C. The importance of water.　　　D. The world's water problem.

第二节　词义搭配：从(B)栏中选出(A)栏单词的正确解释。(共10分,每小题1分)

　　　　A　　　　　　　　　　　B

( )56. typhoon　　　　A. make dirty

( )57. smog　　　　　B. understand, achieve

( )58. sandstorm　　　C. keep safe

( )59. protect　　　　D. smoke and fog

( )60. delay　　　　　E. cars

( )61. realize　　　　F. violent wind

( )62. cancel　　　　 G. sand with wind

( )63. pollute　　　　H. defer

( )64. disaster　　　　I. abandon, stop

( )65. vehicle　　　　J. calamity

第三节 补全对话：根据对话内容，从对话后的选项中选出能填入空白处的最佳选项。(共 10 分, 每小题 2 分)

Jerry: Hi, Mike.It seems that you've got some sunshine.

Mike: I guess so. I spent the weekend on the beach.

Jerry: Really? That sounds exciting. __66__

Mike: At my friend's house. He invited me to stay there as long as I wanted.

Jerry: __67__

Mike: Oh, I have a paper to work on.

Jerry: __68__ I mean besides lying out in the sun.

Mike: I play some volleyball. I never realized how hard it is to run on sand.

Jerry: __69__ Did you go swimming?

Mike: I intended to. __70__ So I just went fishing.

Jerry: All sounds so relaxing

> A. It must be cool.
> B. So what else did you do out there?
> C. Where did you stay?
> D. Then why not stay there for a longer time?
> E. But the water wasn't warm enough.

第三部分 语言技能运用(共分四节 满分 30 分)

第一节 单词拼写：根据下列句子及所给汉语注释,在横线上写出该单词。(共 5 分, 每小题 1 分)

71. The _____（烟雾）makes everything dirty.

72. We went to Tibet to see the _____（自然的）wonder.

73. Please _____（认出,识别,发现）the relationship between natural disasters and human activities.

74. It is possible for us to _____（保护）our earth.

75. Everyone should protect the _____（环境）.

第二节 词形变换：用括号内单词的适当形式填空,将正确答案写在横线上。(共 5 分,每小题 1 分)

76. Waste gases from cars _____ (bad) damaged the air quality.

77. The government have taken some _____ (act) to fight against the pollution.

78. Many things in our life can be recycled and we should _____ (use) it.

Unit 7 Natural Disasters

79. _____ (promote) the use of green energy is important.

80. Natural disasters happen _____ (frequent) than before.

第三节 改错：从 A、B、C、D 四个画线处找出一处错误的选项，并写出正确答案。（共 10 分，每小题 2 分）

81. Where did they hold the important meeting yesterday is unknown to us.
     A   B C   D

82. That the sports meeting will be held is decided by our leader.
  A   B   C D

83. Tom is no longer who he used to be.
    A B C D

84. They do an important job is clear to the public.
  A B   C   D

85. The reason why I was late is because the bus broke down halfway.
      A   B C   D

81. (　　) 应为 _____　　82. (　　) 应为 _____　　83. (　　) 应为 _____

84. (　　) 应为 _____　　85. (　　) 应为 _____

第四节 书面表达（共 10 分）

作文题目：How to Protect our Environment。

词数要求：80~100 词。

写作要点：（1）我们多种树、种花，让我们的城市更美好；

（2）不乱扔垃圾，不倾倒废水；

（3）节约用水；

（4）骑自行车或者步行外出而不是开车；

（5）如果每个人都努力保护环境，我们的城市会变得更美好、更干净。

_____

_____

_____

_____

Unit 8

Role Models of the Times

Warming-up

一、句型汇总

1. We are safe because the police like Ren Changxia are protecting us. 我们安全是因为像任长霞一样的警察在保护我们。

2. I admire doctors like Zhong Nanshan. 我敬佩像钟南山那样的医生。

3. Lang Ping is a respectable volleyball player and coach. 郎平是一位值得尊敬的排球运动员和教练。

二、英汉互译

1. hero _____   2. 冠军_____

3. player _____   4. 消防员_____

5. scientist _____   6. 安全的_____

7. make contributions to _____   8. 敬佩_____

9. devote…to _____   10. 值得尊敬的_____

Unit 8 Role Models of the Times

Listening and Speaking

一、找出与所给单词画线部分读音相同的选项

(   ) 1. aw<u>a</u>rd   A. m<u>a</u>rk   B. c<u>a</u>rtoon   C. w<u>a</u>rn   D. l<u>a</u>rgely

(   ) 2. contr<u>i</u>bution A. l<u>i</u>festyle   B. fac<u>i</u>lity   C. p<u>i</u>rate   D. real<u>i</u>ze

(   ) 3. m<u>a</u>laria   A. c<u>a</u>ncel   B. ch<u>a</u>mpion   C. pr<u>a</u>ctical   D. tr<u>a</u>ditional

(   ) 4. m<u>e</u>dal   A. c<u>e</u>lebrate   B. <u>e</u>ssential   C. <u>e</u>lectric   D. d<u>e</u>lay

(   ) 5. respe<u>c</u>table   A. <u>c</u>raft   B. sin<u>c</u>ere   C. re<u>c</u>eive   D. pra<u>c</u>tice

二、从 B 栏中找出与 A 栏中相对应的答语

A

1. Would you like to watch the tennis match with me this Saturday?
2. Are you still crazy about Yao Ming?
3. I admire your father so much.
4. What do you think of Tu Youyou?
5. How do you plan to realize your dream?

B

A. By working harder.
B. She has contributed a lot to our country.
C. Good idea.
D. My father? Why?
E. Of course. He is my role model.

三、用所给句子补全下面对话

A: Hello. This is Mike.　1　

B: Yes, Tony is speaking.

A: Would you like to play computer games with me?

B: Sorry, I am afraid I can't. I'm reading a piece of news on the newspaper.

A:　2　

B: It's about the meeting held in Beijing on September 8th to commend four role models in the country's fight against the novel coronavirus.

A:　3　

B: They are Zhong Nanshan, Zhang Boli, Zhang Dingyu and Chen Wei.

A:　4　

B: I think they are great for their outstanding contributions to the county's fight against the

COVID-19 epidemic. I want to learn from them.

A: __5__ Let's play basketball to keep healthy!

> A. Who are they?
> B. What is it about?
> C. I agree with you.
> D. Is that Tony speaking?
> E. What do you think of them?

四、场景模拟

编写一组对话。假设你是张丽,和同学杨娟谈论时代楷模张桂梅。

提示词汇：Zhang Guimei/headmaster/title/Role Model of the times/devote…to

_____
_____
_____
_____

Reading and Writing

一、用所给单词的适当形式填空

1. Coming top in the exam was quite an _____ (achieve).
2. He has had another attack of _____ (疟疾).
3. It's an honor to be invited to _____ (contribution) to your magazine.
4. The child smiled at her teacher as he received the _____ (奖励).
5. The drug is not a new _____ (discover) —it has been known about for years.
6. He got a _____ (勋章) for his bravery.
7. The man feels much better after the _____ (treat).
8. He spent his childhood and youth in this _____ (地区).
9. _____ (毫无疑问地), he has made much progress in the six years.
10. Yuan Longping is the "Father of _____ (混合的) Rice."

二、完形填空

What does the power of role models mean to the young? Superstar Su Yiming may be one of the best persons to give a(n) __1__. During the Beijing Winter Olympics, Su became a young idol because he made __2__ in men's snowboard Big Air before his 18th birthday. He not only won two medals but also beat his own idol in the same competition.

Su __3__ young people to try their best to achieve their dreams. "I became interested in snowboarding when I was a kid. And I kept __4__ it. After I knew Beijing would host the 2022 Winter Olympics, I made the Olympics my __5__. I wanted to show the best of myself at the Games," said Su Yiming.

Su only became a professional player about four years ago. But he kept his dream and trained hard for it. "Before the Beijing Winter Games, I had __6__ if I could win, but I achieved my dream of winning a gold medal, so I want to tell the kids that they need to find out the things they __7__ and give them their best efforts. In this way, I believe their dreams will __8__ come true."

Su knew many young people looked up to him as a role model, so he said he couldn't __9__ his progress. "I will try my best to be __10__ for myself and other young people and I will do as much as I can to set a good example for them," Su said.

( ) 1. A. answer   B. activity   C. attendance   D. absence
( ) 2. A. mistakes   B. history   C. money   D. friends
( ) 3. A. invited   B. accepted   C. encouraged   D. changed
( ) 4. A. finding   B. reporting   C. singing   D. practicing
( ) 5. A. lesson   B. dream   C. job   D. business
( ) 6. A. doubts   B. ideas   C. chances   D. regrets
( ) 7. A. share   B. lose   C. love   D. hate
( ) 8. A. suddenly   B. widely   C. highly   D. surely
( ) 9. A. stop   B. make   C. show   D. receive
( ) 10. A. sorry   B. responsible   C. good   D. famous

三、阅读理解

In students' daily life, superstars are usually a hot topic, including their clothes, actions, family members and other things. Who is your favorite superstar? Or you can say who is your role model? Normally the answer to this question can be anyone around you who is excellent. It could also be someone like Zhong Nanshan or Zhang Guimei. They are strong and helpful people.

However, in today's world, teenagers usually look up to pop stars. Teens try to imitate their actions for two main reasons. Firstly, they want to be welcomed by popular culture, and secondly, because stars' actions are so well reported by the media that everyone wants to follow stars' lifestyles.

These days, some reports about stars are surprising. Some smoke or some drive after drinking. So they have to say sorry after being caught doing bad things. Others even say bad words about their family members. These bad actions or lifestyles are inappropriate for teenagers.

In fact, some people believe that teenagers can try to be a good role model themselves. Even if they are not famous people, they can still be role models to their sisters, brothers, and younger neighbors.

What's more, teenagers should use their good eyes to find good examples around them, like soldiers who protect our motherland, like doctors and nurses who take care of the patients with COVID-19 while they may be in danger themselves. From their words and actions, you can improve yourselves, so that the power of examples can shock every heart around us!

( )1. According to the first paragraph, _____ people should be role models.

  A. rich   B. beautiful   C. helpful   D. lazy

( )2. What are the main reasons for the teens to imitate stars?

  A. They hope to be rich.

  B. They hope to be welcomed and follow stars' lifestyles.

  C. They hope to be fashionable and popular.

  D. Their parents ask them to do so.

( )3. The underlined word "inappropriate" in Paragraph 3 means _____.

  A. 不恰当的   B. 不确定的   C. 不奇怪的   D. 不重要的

( )4. Who are the good examples for teenagers?

  A. Superstars who drive after drinking.

  B. Sisters, brothers, and younger neighbors.

  C. Fashionable people around us.

  D. Soldiers who protect our motherland.

( )5. The writer wants teenagers to _____.

  A. learn how to be welcomed and popular

  B. learn how to choose right role models

  C. learn how to follow pop stars' steps

  D. learn how to become popular stars

Unit 8 Role Models of the Times

四、书面表达

你校英文校刊正组织以"榜样的力量"为主题的征文活动。请你用英语写一篇短文投稿，介绍你心中的一位榜样以及你欣赏他（她）的理由。

1. 提示词汇：role model/hard-working/helpful/make important contributions to/learn from

2. 写作要点：（1）榜样的事迹；

（2）你欣赏他（她）的理由等。

3. 注意事项：（1）文中不得出现考生个人真实信息；

（2）词数 80~100 词；

（3）开头已给出，不计入总词数。

My Role Model

Role models make a difference to us. _____

_____

_____

_____

_____

Grammar

一、从下面每小题四个选项中选出最佳选项

(　　) 1. _____ more attention, the trees could have grown better.

A. Having given　　B. Giving　　C. Given　　D. To give

(　　) 2. _____ by the beauty of nature, the girl from England decided to spend two days on the farm.

A. To attract　　B. Attracted　　C. Attracting　　D. Attracts

(　　) 3. _____ anything about the accident, he went to work as usual.

A. Not knowing　　B. Not known　　C. Knowing not　　D. Known not

(　　) 4. While _____ TV, we heard the doorbell ring.

A. watched　　B. watches　　C. to watch　　D. watching

(　　) 5. I'm sorry I was late. _____ up for it, let me treat you to a meal.

A. Making　　B. To make　　C. Made　　D. Make

(   )6. Mr. Yang gets up very early every morning _____ the early bus.

    A. to catch   B. catching   C. caught   D. catch

(   )7. _____ from the hill, the city looks beautiful.

    A. Seeing   B. See   C. To see   D. Seen

(   )8. The students walked into the office, _____ their teacher.

    A. followed   B. followed by   C. following   D. following by

(   )9. We are looking for a good place _____ the welcome party.

    A. hold   B. to hold   C. holding   D. held

(   )10. It's really dangerous to use your phone when _____.

    A. drive   B. drove   C. driven   D. driving

(   )11. _____ enough time, the Smiths spent their holidays at home last year.

    A. Not having   B. Not have   C. Not had   D. Having not

(   )12. We should always treat everyone with kindness and warmth, _____ love and joy.

    A. spread   B. spreads   C. spreading   D. to spread

(   )13. When I was young, I liked to listen to the radio, _____ for my favorite song.

    A. waited   B. waiting   C. to wait   D. waits

(   )14. He has no time _____ his homework.

    A. do   B. doing   C. done   D. to do

(   )15. All the things _____, she has done very well.

    A. considered   B. considering   C. to consider   D. considers

(   )16. Some boys were on the playground _____ basketball.

    A. play   B. plays   C. playing   D. played

(   )17. The old woman went into the room, _____ by his daughter.

    A. supporting   B. supported   C. to support   D. supports

(   )18. The man sits in front of the television every day, _____ everything that is happening at home and abroad.

    A. watching   B. to watch   C. watched   D. watches

(   )19. I will write down your telephone number so as _____ it.

    A. not forgetting   B. not forget   C. not to forget   D. not forgotten

(   )20. _____ around, the students listened to the story in detail.

    A. Stood   B. Standing   C. Stand   D. To stand

(   )21. The test _____, we began our holiday.

A. finishing   B. to finish   C. has finished   D. finished

( )22. _____ the news, he jumped up.

A. Hearing   B. To hear   C. Hear   D. Heard

( )23. I think I'm so lucky _____ such a good teacher.

A. have   B. to have   C. having   D. had

( )24. _____ by car, we visited many exciting and beautiful places.

A. Travel   B. Travels   C. Traveled   D. Traveling

( )25. The students went out of the classroom, _____.

A. laugh and singing   B. laughing and sing

C. laughing and singing   D. laugh and sing

( )26. They worked harder than usual in order _____ the task on time.

A. to finish   B. finishing   C. finished   D. finishes

( )27. _____ why she did it, the girl said it was her duty.

A. Asking   B. Asks   C. Ask   D. Asked

( )28. When _____ a post office, I stopped to buy some stamps.

A. passing   B. passed   C. passes   D. to pass

( )29. _____ more, the flowers could have grown better.

A. To water   B. Waters   C. Watered   D. Watering

( )30. He is not old enough _____ this job.

A. do   B. to do   C. doing   D. done

二、根据要求转换句子

1. When they heard the news, they jumped with joy.（改为简单句）

_____ _____ _____, they jumped with joy.

2. After he returned home, he began to work.（改为非谓语动词作状语）

_____ _____ home, he began to work.

3. While we are walking along the river, we heard someone shouting.（改为简单句）

_____ along the river, we heard someone shouting.

4. He got up early so that he could catch the train.（改为目的状语）

He got up early _____ _____ the train.

5. The boy is so young that he can't go to school.（改为同义句）

The boy is not _____ _____ _____ go to school.

6. Because she was ill, she couldn't go to school.（改为简单句）

_____ _____, she couldn't go to school.

7. He is such a strong man that he can carry the heavy box. (改为简单句)

   He is _____ enough _____ carry the heavy box.

8. As he was born in Shanghai, he knew the city very well. (改为非谓语动词作状语)

   _____ in Shanghai, he knew the city very well.

9. Because we didn't know his address, we couldn't get in touch with him. (改为简单句)

   _____ _____ his address, we couldn't get in touch with him.

10. He stood on the rock in order that we could see him clearly. (改为简单句)

    He stood on the rock _____ us _____ _____ him clearly.

For Better Performance

一、找出与所给单词画线部分读音相同的选项

( ) 1. achieve　　A. change　　B. chemistry　　C. character　　D. technology

( ) 2. champion　　A. global　　B. locate　　C. cancel　　D. allow

( ) 3. contribution　　A. location　　B. improve　　C. complaint　　D. properly

( ) 4. discovery　　A. check　　B. discover　　C. especially　　D. essential

( ) 5. drug　　A. reduce　　B. solution　　C. refund　　D. regular

二、英汉互译

1. award _____　　2. 基本的,关键的 _____

3. discovery _____　　4. 荣誉,辉煌 _____

5. lead _____　　6. 勋章 _____

7. look up to _____　　8. 值得尊敬的 _____

9. succeed in doing sth. _____　　10. 楷模 _____

三、用所给单词的适当形式填空

1. There is nobody who doesn't _____ (敬佩) him.

2. Zhang Fuqing has made great _____ (contribute) to our country.

3. The boys competed with each other for the _____ (奖励).

4. We joined a _____ (profession) organization for writers.

Unit 8 Role Models of the Times

5. My mother is a _____ (respect) woman.

6. He held the title of world _____ (冠军) for three years.

7. It's an _____ (基本的,关键的) thing in life.

8. My two brothers are both _____ (消防员).

9. More than 20 watches are not up to _____ (标准).

10. A coach should act as a _____ (模范) for his athletes.

四、找出下列句子中错误的选项,并改正过来

1. We are <u>safety</u> because <u>the police</u> <u>are</u> protecting <u>us</u>.
             A   B   C   D

2. <u>Your</u> role model is <u>one of</u> the <u>model</u> of the <u>times</u>.
     A   B   C   D

3. I <u>want to</u> be a teacher like you, <u>helping</u> kids <u>become</u> great people when they <u>growth</u> up.
      A   B   C   D

4. Yuan Longping <u>successfully</u> developed a <u>special</u> type of rice, <u>put</u> China in the global lead <u>in</u> rice production.
                     A   B   C
   D

5. The crop <u>is</u> now <u>grown</u> in <u>more</u> than 30 <u>country</u> and regions.
            A   B   C   D

1.( ) 应为_____ 2.( ) 应为_____ 3.( ) 应为_____
4.( ) 应为_____ 5.( ) 应为_____

单元检测

第一部分 英语知识运用(共分三节,满分40分)

第一节 语音知识: 从 A、B、C、D 四个选项中找出其画线部分与所给单词画线部分读音相同的选项。(共5分,每小题1分)

( )1. ess<u>e</u>ntial   A. caf<u>e</u>teria   B. <u>e</u>specially   C. repr<u>e</u>sent   D. s<u>e</u>ction

( )2. l<u>ea</u>d   A. d<u>ea</u>th   B. br<u>ea</u>th   C. tr<u>ea</u>tment   D. <u>a</u>rea

( )3. pr<u>i</u>ze   A. l<u>i</u>festyle   B. d<u>i</u>saster   C. r<u>i</u>sk   D. del<u>i</u>very

( )4. st<u>a</u>ndard   A. sm<u>a</u>rt   B. d<u>a</u>rk   C. l<u>a</u>rge   D. sol<u>a</u>r

( )5. pr<u>o</u>fessional   A. v<u>o</u>lcano   B. w<u>o</u>nder   C. c<u>o</u>ntribute   D. sm<u>o</u>g

— 137 —

第二节 词汇与语法知识：从 A、B、C、D 四个选项中选出可以填入空白处的最佳选项。(共 25 分,每小题 1 分)

(　　) 6. Yang Kezhang, a hero who lost his life for _____ people from a fire.
   A. save   B. saved   C. saves   D. saving

(　　) 7. Ren Changxia has devoted her life _____ the cause of people's safety.
   A. to   B. on   C. of   D. in

(　　) 8. Lang Ping is a _____ volleyball player and coach.
   A. comfortable B. respectable C. available D. enjoyable

(　　) 9. I like science very much and want to be a _____ like Qian Xuesen.
   A. doctor B. businessman C. scientist D. firefighter

(　　) 10. Many of my classmates are _____ of different players.
   A. fans   B. coaches   C. teachers   D. parents

(　　) 11. I admire the police who protect us and keep us _____.
   A. safety   B. safe   C. safely   D. security

(　　) 12. My friend is _____ Yao Ming and his teammates.
   A. bad for B. good for C. good at D. crazy about

(　　) 13. Yuan Longping _____ developed a special type of rice with a high yield.
   A. success B. successful C. successfully D. succeed

(　　) 14. I'd like to be a professional tennis player, _____ glory for our country.
   A. win   B. wins   C. won   D. winning

(　　) 15. Their success can encourage the young to go for their dreams and _____ the world.
   A. contribute to B. contribute C. contributions to D. contribution

(　　) 16. Tu Youyou and her workmates studied ancient Chinese medicine books and different traditional _____.
   A. treatment B. treatments C. treat D. treats

(　　) 17. When I wanted to _____, your deeds gave me the confidence and courage.
   A. look up B. turn up C. give up D. get up

(　　) 18. We always _____ scientists, such as Yuan Longping, Tu Youyou and Yu Min.
   A. look into B. look after C. look for D. look up to

(　　) 19. I will do what I can _____ people, like Ren Changxia.
   A. to protect B. protect C. protecting D. protected

(　　) 20. —Would you like to go to watch the basketball match with me this Sunday?

—_____.

    A. That's right   B. You're welcome

    C. Good idea   D. Take it easy

(　　)21. Thanks to Tu's contribution, more than 240 _____ Africans have benefited.

    A. millions   B. million   C. millions of   D. million of

(　　)22. _____ in the shopping mall, I met a friend of mine.

    A. To walk   B. Walks   C. Walked   D. Walking

(　　)23. Yuan Longping set world records in hybrid rice yields in many years, _____ a solution to worldwide hunger.

    A. providing   B. provided   C. provide   D. provides

(　　)24. While window shopping, she _____ her old classmates.

    A. came out   B. came true   C. came across   D. came from

(　　)25. _____ nearly 200 experiments, they finally succeeded in getting artemisinin.

    A. Doing   B. Having done   C. To do   D. Done

(　　)26. I was deeply _____ by Yuan Longping's love and care for the people.

    A. move   B. movement   C. moved   D. moving

(　　)27. _____ equal chances, both of them can finish the task.

    A. Given   B. Give   C. Gives   D. Gave

(　　)28. After so _____ research, his dream came true.

    A. much years of   B. much years

    C. many years   D. many years of

(　　)29. _____ in thought, he almost ran into the car in front of him.

    A. Lose   B. Lost   C. Loses   D. Losing

(　　)30. _____ that millions of people benefited from his medical project.

    A. It said   B. It saying   C. It's said   D. It's saying

第三节　完形填空：阅读下面的短文，从所给的 A、B、C、D 四个选项中选出最佳的答案。(共 10 分，每小题 1 分)

    I am as proud of my Chinese heritage and background as I am devoted to modern science, a part of human civilization of Western origin. —Yang Zhenning

    For the past 20 years, the Touching China annual people __31__ has honored people from all walks of life across the country. They are people __32__ warm our hearts with their actions. This year, 10 inspirational role models were __33__ the list.

    Let's get to know one of them, Yang Zhenning, who is a 99 year-old famous physicist. He was

  __34__ for making great contributions to physics.

  No matter where he has been, Yang Zhenning has always had his motherland in mind. In1957, Yang was studying in the US. He and another Chinese student, Tsung-dao Lee（李政道）, __35__ a physics theory together. Months later, the two won the Nobel Prize in Physics for their theory. Their achievement __36__ that Chinese scientists could be on the global world.

  __37__, the "frozen" Sino-US relations（中美关系）prevented Chinese scientists who received doctoral degrees（博士学位）in the US from __38__ to China.

  Then, in 1971, Yang finally got the __39__ to return to China for a visit. Later, Yang sold a house in the US, donating the money to Tsinghua University. In 2003, Yang returned to China and also taught in Tsinghua.

  Under his leadership, many overseas Chinese students returned to China to make contributions, __40__ Turing Award winner Yao Qizhi and physics Wu Xiaogang.

  (　　)31. A. forward   B. reward   C. award   D. toward
  (　　)32. A. whom   B. who   C. whose   D. which
  (　　)33. A. on   B. of   C. to   D. in
  (　　)34. A. choose   B. chose   C. chosen   D. choosing
  (　　)35. A. came up with   B. came true   C. came over   D. comes true
  (　　)36. A. protected   B. produced   C. provided   D. proved
  (　　)37. A. But   B. However   C. Therefore   D. Instead
  (　　)38. A. return   B. returns   C. returned   D. returning
  (　　)39. A. money   B. change   C. chance   D. idea
  (　　)40. A. such as   B. for example   C. instead of   D. because of

第二部分　篇章与词汇理解(共分三节,满分50分)

第一节　阅读理解：阅读下列短文,从每题所给A、B、C、D四个选项中选出最恰当的答案。(共30分,每小题2分)

A

  Many people have made great contributions to our country's development. Eight of them received Medal of Republic on October 1 st, 2019. They are national heroes. Now let's learn about four of them.

Yu Min（1926-2019）
Nuclear（核能的）physicist
On June 17, 1967, China detonated（引爆）its first hydrogen bomb（氢弹）. It took only 32 months to go from its first atom bomb（原子弹）to its first hydrogen bomb. As a nuclear physicist, YuMin played an important role in this process. His theories（理论）and models were the key to the successful test.

Unit 8　Role Models of the Times

ZhangFuqing（1924-）
War veteran（老兵）
Zhang was a soldier in the People's Liberation Army during the Liberation War. He was twice presented the title of Combat Hero（战斗英雄）. In 1955, he volunteered to work in a remote（偏远的）county in Hubei Province and has been helping poor people there ever since.
Yuan Longping（1930-2021）
"Father of hybrid rice"
Yuan spent his whole life in agricultural education and research. He is the first person in the world to develop a hybrid rice strain（杂交水稻品种）. His research on higher rice yields（产量）helps fight hunger in China and other parts of the world.
Tu Youyou（1930-）
Scientist
Tu is known for winning the Nobel Prize in Physiology or Medicine in 2015. She got <u>inspiration</u> from traditional Chinese medicine theories and discovered artemisinin（青蒿素）, a medicine that can be used to treat malaria（疟疾）. Her finding has saved the lives of millions.

(　　)41. China's first atom was detonated in _____.
　　A. October, 1964　　　　B. December, 1963
　　C. June, 1965　　　　　D. July, 1962

(　　)42. Which of the following is true about Zhang Fuqing?
　　A. He has always been a soldier.
　　B. He became a combat hero twice.
　　C. Hewas sent to work in a remote country in 1955.
　　D. He once worked in Hebei Province and helped poor people there.

(　　)43. Yuan Longping is known as "Father of hybrid rice" because _____.
　　A. he is the second person to develop a hybrid rice strain
　　B. he bought the hybrid rice
　　C. he discovered the hybrid rice strain
　　D. he developed a hybrid rice strain

(　　)44. The underlined word "inspiration" in the last paragraph means _____.
　　A. 灵魂　　　B. 秘诀　　　C. 灵感　　　D. 智慧

(　　)45. The purpose of this passage is to _____.
　　A. make people remember them and learn from them
　　B. encourage people to be heroes like them
　　C. explain reasons why they want to do that
　　D. introduce the hybrid rice strain to people

B

Liu Xiuxiang was born in a poor family. When he was 4, his father died. His mother developed mental health problems. When he was 10, his elder brother and sisters left and never returned. To make a living, Liu collected rubbish, and in high school he worked 18 hours a day during summer vacations. However difficult it was, he never gave up his study.

In 2007, Liu failed the exam to university. He got confused. He wondered if he should continue studying. After working in a bathhouse for about 50 days, he decided to go back to school. In 2008, he finally passed the exam and went to university.

After graduation, he became a history teacher in his hometown. "I want to come back to tell the children, who are as poor and lost as I was, that education has changed my life." Liu set a good example for them to take control of lives through education.

Now Liu gives speeches around the country. His story inspires many students and encourages people to help those from poor families. Since 2012, he has helped more than 1,900 students and called on more teachers to work in poor areas to improve the quality of education.

Liu was titled "the most beautiful teacher" in 2020. His story moves us a lot.

(　　)46. Liu Xiuxiang worked _____ hours a day during summer vacations in high school.
　　　　A. eighty-eight　　B. eighteen　　C. eighty　　D. eighth

(　　)47. The underlined word "confused" in Paragraph 2 means _____.
　　　　A. 困难的　　B. 迷路的　　C. 错过的　　D. 困惑的

(　　)48. Liu was titled "the most beautiful teacher" in _____.
　　　　A. 2007　　B. 2008　　C. 2012　　D. 2020

(　　)49. Which of the following is not true accprding to the passage?
　　　　A. Liu decided to go back to school after working in a bathhouse.
　　　　B. Liu became a history teacher and set a good example.
　　　　C. Liu's story inspires all the students and encourages people to help those from poor families.
　　　　D. Liu called on more teachers to work in poor areas to improve the quality of education.

(　　)50. The passageis written in the order of _____.
　　　　A. time　　B. space　　C. person　　D. opinions

C

On Sept. 8, 2020, President Xi Jinping presents medals to the recipient（接受者）of the Medal of the Republic Zhong Nanshan, and recipients of the national honorary title "the People's

Unit 8 Role Models of the Times

Hero," Zhang Boli, Zhang Dingyu and Chen Wei, at a meeting commending (表彰) role models in the country's fight against the COVID-19 epidemic (流行病) at the Great Hall of the People in Beijing.

Zhong Nanshan is one of them. He led his team to Wuhan to fight against the illness. He made the important decision to cut off Wuhan from other cities to stop the virus. Thanks to him, the disease is under control day by day.

"Wearing this uniform, I should do everything for the country," said Chen Wei, a key figure behind the vaccine (疫苗). She made great achievements in COVID-19 related basic research and development of vaccine and protective medicine.

Zhang Dingyu, head of Wuhan Jinyintan Hospital, learned that his wife was infected (感染) with COVID-19, but he still fought in the front line of the epidemic for more than 30 days. And he led the medical team to treat thousands of patients.

Although people have different positions, industries, abilities and levels, they can create great achievements in common positions. That's because they have heroic dreams and do heroic deeds. Everyone <u>admires</u> a hero. The heroic Chinese people will surely create newer and greater Chinese miracles (奇迹).

(　　) 51. Which of the following is true about Zhang Dingyu?

　　A. He fought in the front line of the epidemic for less than 30 days.

　　B. His son was infected (感染) with COVID-19.

　　C. His medical team saved thousands of patients.

　　D. He worked in Jiangsu.

(　　) 52. According to the passage, the recipients are honored because they are all _____.

　　A. the role models in the country's fight against the COVID-19 epidemic

　　B. making great achievements in science

　　C. key figures behind the vaccine

　　D. developing vaccine and protective medicine in 2020

(　　) 53. What mainly makes common people create great achievements according to the passage?

　　A. High positions.　　　　　　　　B. Good abilities and high levels.

　　C. Heroic dreams and do heroic deeds.　　D. Great feelings.

(　　) 54. The underlined word "admires" in the last Paragraph means _____.

　　A. looks down upon　　B. loves　　C. imagines　　D. looks up to

(　　) 55. What's the best title for the passage?

　　A. Development of Vaccine　　　　B. Give the Epidemic Heroes Thumbs up

C. China's Great Achievements　　D. The Heroic Dreams of People

第二节　词义搭配：从(B)栏中选出(A)栏单词的正确解释。(共10分,每小题1分)

A　　　　　　　　　　　　　　B

(　　)56. admire　　　　A. the action of accomplishing something

(　　)57. discovery　　　B. an award for winning a championship

(　　)58. firefighter　　C. the quantity of something that is created

(　　)59. medal　　　　D. a substance that is used as a medicine or narcotic

(　　)60. achievement　　E. the act of discovering something

(　　)61. player　　　　F. the extended spatial location of something

(　　)62. output　　　　G. a person who participates in or is skilled at some games

(　　)63. drug　　　　　H. of or relating to or suitable as a profession

(　　)64. region　　　　I. feel admiration for

(　　)65. professional　　J. a member of a fire department who tries to extinguish fires

第三节　补全对话：根据对话内容,从对话后的选项中选出能填入空白处的最佳选项。(共10分,每小题2分)

A：Hi, Jessica. I called you yesterday evening but nobody answered. ___66___

B：I'm sorry, Linda. I was watching an interview with Zhong Nanshan by Xinhua news agency.

A：Wow. I admire him very much. ___67___

B：I think he is great. Although he is in his eighties, he is still very serious about work.

A：I agree with you. Whom did you watch the interview with?

B：___68___ We were all deeply moved by the spirit of Zhong Nanshan.

A：Right, he has made great achievements in medicine.

B：That's true. ___69___

A：How are you going to realize it?

B：By studying hard. Now I am going to borrow some medical books from the library. ___70___

A：Yes, I'd love to. Let's go.

　　A. What do you think of him?
　　B. Would you like to go there with me?
　　C. With my parents.
　　D. What were you doing at that time?
　　E. I want to be a doctor like him in the future.

Unit 8 Role Models of the Times

第三部分　语言技能应用(共分四节,满分30分)

第一节　单词拼写：根据下列句子及所给汉语注释在横线上写出该单词。(共5分,每小题1分)

71. I work as a _____ (消防员) and my wife is a nurse.

72. The little boy got a _____ (勋章) for his bravery.

73. The old man tried every _____ (治疗) the doctor suggested.

74. We all _____ (敬佩) him for his honesty.

75. There is no absolute _____ (标准) for beauty.

第二节　词形变换：用括号内单词的适当形式填空,将正确答案写在横线上。(共5分,每小题1分)

76. He has made important _____ (contribute) to the company's success.

77. I felt a great sense of _____ (achieve) when I reached the top of the mountain.

78. New scientific _____ (discover) are made every day.

79. Yao Ming is a famous basketball _____ (play).

80. Don't wear those clothes to work. Try to look more _____ (profession).

第三节　改错：从A、B、C、D四个画线处找出一处错误的选项,并写出正确答案。(共10分,每小题2分)

81. Tu Youyou <u>is</u> <u>the first</u> Chinese scientist <u>winning</u> the Nobel Prize <u>in</u> Medicine.
　　　　　　 A　　B　　　　　　　　　　　　　C　　　　　　　　　D

82. Thanks <u>for</u> Tu's contribution, more than 240 <u>million</u> people <u>in</u> Africa <u>have</u> benefited.
　　　　　 A　　　　　　　　　　　　　　　　　 B　　　　　C　　　　　D

83. Their <u>success</u> can encourage <u>the</u> young <u>to</u> go for their dreams and <u>contribute</u> the world.
　　　　　 A　　　　　　　　　　 B　　　　 C　　　　　　　　　　　　　　　D

84. <u>For</u> more than 60 years, he <u>deliberate</u> kept <u>his</u> past <u>achievements</u> a secret.
　　 A　　　　　　　　　　　　 B　　　　　　　C　　　　　D

85. <u>One of them</u> <u>is</u> Yuan Longping, <u>known</u> <u>for</u> the "Father of Hybrid Rice".
　　 A　　　　 B　　　　　　　　　　 C　　　 D

81. (　　)应为_____　82. (　　)应为_____　83. (　　)应为_____
84. (　　)应为_____　85. (　　)应为_____

第四节　书面表达(共10分)

榜样的力量是无穷的。为了更好地发挥榜样的引领作用,学校下周计划举行以"The Heart in My Heart"为主题的英语演讲比赛。请你写一篇演讲稿,介绍一下自己心目中的英雄。

1. 提示词：influence/work hard/try one's best/devote one's life to/impress

145

2. 写作要点：(1)英雄的事迹；

(2)你喜欢他(她)的原因等。

3. 注意事项：(1)文中不得出现考生个人真实信息；

(2)词数 80~100 词；

(3)开头已给出，不计入总词数。

The Hero in My Heart

Heroes have a great influence on our life.

参考答案

Unit 1　Festivals Around The World

Warming-up

二、1. 欣赏　2. 标志　符号　3. 表现　4. 装饰　5. 壁炉　6. receive　7. playful　8. craft　9. gala　10. reunion

Listening and Speaking

一、1. A　2. D　3. B　4. A　5. B

二、1. C　2. D　3. B　4. E　5. A

三、1. B　2. C　3. D　4. E　5. A

四、场景模拟

A：The Spring Festival is drawing close. By then we will have five days off. I am expecting it.

B：Can you tell me something about the Spring Festival?

A：Just like you celebrate Christmas, we celebrate our lunar New Year's Day, the Spring Festival, It's the beginning of the next year. It is a time for the family members and relatives to have a get-together.

B：What are the children doing?

A：They usually go outside to play firecrackers and fireworks. At 24 hours midnight, the time when the New Year real comes, we exchange "Happy New Year" to each other, and parents and grandparents will take out small packages wrapped with red paper, in them are some what we call "Lucky Money".

B：Who will get the money?

A：Of course the children.

Reading and Writing

一、1. gala   2. similar   3. Nowadays   4. performance   5. racing
   6. snacks   7. symbol   8. crafts   9. respection   10. decoration

二、1. B 2. B 3. C 4. D 5. A 6. C 7. A 8. B 9. C 10. D

三、1. B 2. A 3. A 4. A 5. C

四、书面表达

Mid Autumn Festival is a traditional festival of China. It used to be as important as Spring Festival. it is usually celebrated in September or October. This festival is to celebrate the harvest and to enjoy the beautiful moonlight. To some extent it is like Thanksgiving day in western countries. On this day people usually get together with their families and have nice meal，after that people always eat delicious moon cakes and watch the moon. The moon is always very round on that day and makes people think of their relatives and friends. It is a day of pleasure and happiness. Hope you have a wonderful Mid Autumn Festival.

Grammar

一、1. C 2. A 3. D 4. A 5. B 6. B 7. C 8. B 9. D 10. A
   11. D 12. D 13. C 14. B 15. A 16. D 17. C 18. D 19. B 20. A
   21. A 22. D 23. D 24. B 25. A 26. A 27. C 28. C 29. A 30. C

二、1. B 改成 be   2. B 改成 some   3. A 改成 read   4. A 改成 little   5. B 改成 going
   6. B 改成 careful   7. B 改成 welcomed   8. B 改成 to go   9. C 改成 to order
   10. B 改成 flying

For Better Performance

一、1. D 2. C 3. A 4. D 5. B

二、1. 落到 2. 与……相同 3. 收到你的邀请 4. 敲击 5. 不招待就使坏
   6. at the beginning of   7. prefer doing   8. Santa Claus   9. wash away
   10. at the end of

三、1. keeping   2. speaking   3. to do   4. not to be   5. forgot   6. going   7. to receive

8. to remember　9. joining　10. listen

四、1. A 改成 lived　2. A 改成 on　3. D 改成 for　4. C 改成 from　5. D 改成 with

单元检测

第一部分　英语知识运用

第一节　1. B　2. C　3. C　4. D　5. D

第二节　6. A　7. B　8. C　9. B　10. D　11. D　12. A　13. B　14. A　15. C
16. B　17. D　18. C　19. A　20. B　21. C　22. C　23. B　24. D　25. D
26. C　27. C　28. D　29. B　30. D

第三节　31. A　32. A　33. C　34. C　35. B　36. A　37. D　38. C　39. D　40. C

第二部分　篇章与词汇理解

第一节　41. B　42. C　43 D　44. B　45. A　46. D　47. C　48. D　49. A　50. D
51. D　52. B　53. C　54. A　55. A

第二节　56. B　57. C　58. I　59. H　60. J　61. D　62. E　63. F　64. A　65. G

第三节　66. C　67. E　68. B　69. D　70. A

第三部分　语言技能运用

第一节　71. playful　72. moon cakes　73. symbol　74. reunion　75. crafts

第二节　76. to rebuild　77. annoyed　78. cheerful　79. interviewers　80. freedom

第三节　81. A 改成 Follow　82. B 改成 moves　83. B 改成 watching　84. C 改成 drive
85. B 改成 not being

第四节　书面表达(共10分)

The Dragon Boat Festival, also called the Duanwu Festival, is celebrated on the fifth day of the fifth month according to the Chinese calendar. This festival is to commemorate the death of QuYuan.The most important activity of this festival is the Dragon Boat races. It symbolizes people's attempts to rescue Qu Yuan. In the current period, these races also demonstrate the virtues of cooperation and teamwork. Besides, the festival has also been marked by eating Zong zi. People who mourned the death of Qu Yuan threw Zong zi into the river to feed his ghost every year.

Although the significance of the festival might be different with the past, it still gives the observer an opportunity to glimpse a part of the rich Chinese cultural heritage.

Unit 2 Community Life

Warming-up

二、1. 便利店 2. 社区 3. facility 4. 邻居 5. purpose 6. 对立的 7. 药品
    8. 交通 9. laundry 10. 环境 11. cinema 12. location 13. 重要的 14. suit

Listening and Speaking

一、1. D 2. B 3. B 4. C 5. B

二、1. C 2. B 3. D 4. E 5. A

三、1. B 2. D 3. E 4. A 5. C

四、场景模拟

A：What kind of apartment would you like?

B：I'd like a house near the country. In that case, we can enjoy the fresh air every day.

A：What about the size?

B：I prefer a double-room apartment.

A：This apartment is just suitable for you, and there are many facilities in this community.

B：Is there a shop in the community?

A：Yes, There is a convenience store、a clinic、a beauty salon in the community.

B：Oh, thank you very much.

Reading and Writing

一、1. nearest 2. minutes' 3. to live 4. to find 5. more important
    6. to share 7. watching 8. will know 9. located 10. attracting

二、1. B 2. C 3. A 4. D 5. C 6. A 7. B 8. A 9. C 10. B

三、1. B 2. A 3. C 4. D 5. B

四、书面表达

My dream neighborhood is in the center of city. It's a great place to live. Because if offers us a convenient life which everybody dreams of. It's a very busy and clean area. There are lots of cars on Center Street, especially in the morning and evening. Because most people travel at those two time periods. And it is full of clean area because of the beautiful flowers and green trees. In addition, there is a big supermarket near my house where I can buy almost everything I need in my daily life. Besides, some restaurants are located by my house, in which I can eat different types of food anytime I want. Moreover, there is a playground or beautiful garden where kids can play and old man can dance happily. Next to the garden is a gym and there is a swimming poor inside it. I can work out in my spare time.

It's a really great neighborhood. Welcome to my dream neighborhood.

Grammar

一、1. A 2. A 3. C 4. A 5. A 6. D 7. A 8. D 9. C 10. D

11. D 12. B 13. C 14. A 15. C 16. B 17. D 18. C 19. A 20. A

21. D 22. A 23. D 24. B 25. B 26. B 27. D 28. C 29. B 30. D

二、1. C 改成 first   2. C 改成 whose   3. B 改成 wich   4. C 改成 been built

5. C 改成 where   6. 去掉 D   7. D 改成 comfortably   8. C 改成 snowed it   9. A 改成 so

10. C 改成 as

For Better Performance

一、1. D 2. B 3. B 4. A 5. B

二、1. 熟悉   2. 在……对面   3. 购物商场   4. 代替   5. 美容院   6. 有机会

7. 健身房   8. convenience store   9. check out   10. meet one's need

三、1. buy   2. shop   3. moved   4. be found   5. suitable

6. perfectly   7. to find   8. reading   9. swimming   10. Chinese

四、1. D 改成 terrible   2. B 改成 that   3. D 改成 home   4. B 改成 which   5. C 改成 which

单元检测

第一部分　英语知识运用

第一节　1. B　2. D　3. A　4. D　5. C

第二节　6. B　7. D　8. A　9. D　10. C　11. A　12. D　13. D　14. A　15. C
16. B　17. B　18. D　19. A　20. C　21. D　22. B　23. C　24. C　25. B
26. B　27. C　28. B　29. B　30. D

第三节　31. D　32. C　33. B　34. D　35. C　36. A　37. C　38. A　39. B　40. B

第二部分　篇章与词汇理解

第一节　41. D　42. A　43. C　44. B　45. B　46. B　47. C　48. D　49. C　50. B
51. D　52. B　53. D　54. C　55. C

第二节　56. J　57. F　58. E　59. D　60. C　61. B　62. A　63. G　64. I　65. H

第三节　66. B　67. E　68. A　69. C　70. D

第三部分　语言技能运用

第一节　71. facility　72. gym　73. laundry　74. lifestyle　75. purpose

第二节　76. teeth　77. takes　78. getting　79. interesting　80. twice

第三节　81. B 改成 where　82. B 改成 be allowed　83. B 改成 pronunciation
84. C 改成 making　85. C 改成 difference

第四节　书面表达(共10分)

　　I live in a community on Yu Hua Road. Around it there are supermarkets, restaurants, a school and a hospital. The community is very beautiful, and the flowers, plants and trees are slowly increasing. There is a wide playground in the middle of the community, which is children's paradise. Children can ride a car and slide a pulley happily on it. The neighbors here are very kind and helpful. Some of them are volunteers. They often meet at the community center and share their different skills. They can help people with all kinds of problems. At the weekend they usually have a "helping hands" meeting. Then they help people check their computers or fix their bicycles. Sometimes they also visit old people and help them do some shopping or clean their flats. I think we're lucky to live in a community like this.

Unit 3　Artificial Intelligence

Warming-up

二、1. communicate　2. disaster　3. education　4. improve　5. obvious
　　6. properly　7. 优势　8. 态度　9. 利益　10. 风险　11. 效率　12. 服务

Listening and Speaking

一、1. D　2. B　3. C　4. A　5. B

二、1. B　2. E　3. D　4. A　5. C

三、1. D　2. B　3. E　4. C　5. A

四、

Wang Mei：Hello, Li Lei, do you know AI ?

Li Lei：Sure, it's used in many fields now.

Wang Mei：Do you think it's a good thing or a bad thing?

Li Lei：I think it's a good thing. It can change our lives, it also can free people from heavy work.

Wang Mei：But I don't agree with you. I think AI may cause many people losing their jobs. I'm afraid AI may take place of human being.

Li Lei：You needn't worry, it's human design and control robots. AI can help lower cost and save time. If we can make good use of it, it will benefit us in many fields instead of losing control.

Wang Mei：Perhaps you are right.

Reading and Writing

一、1. application　2. benefit　3. efficiency　4. assembly　5. advantage
　　6. applied　7. cause　8. disaster　9. increasing　10. obvious

二、1. D　2. B　3. A　4. C　5. D　6. A　7. D　8. B　9. B　10. C

三、1. B 2. C 3. B 4. A 5. D

四、

AI and our life

With the development of science and technology, AI is used widely in our daily life. For example, it can be used in department store, education, transportation, factories, restaurant and so on. It changes the way we live and work. I think it helps people a lot with their lives. Take the mobile payment as an example, it is more convenient than the traditional payment methods. People needn't worry about losing their money and it also saves time. So in my opinion, AI is very useful if we can make good use of it. It must be a promising new thing in the future.

Grammar

一、1. C 2. C 3. D 4. D 5. B 6. B 7. A 8. B 9. C 10. C
　　11. C 12. C 13. A 14. C 15. B 16. A 17. D 18. B 19. A 20. A
　　21. A 22. C 23. C 24. C 25. C 26. A 27. D 28. C 29. B 30. C

二、1. C 改为 to save   2. A 改为 made   3. B 改为 talking   4. A 改为 written
　　5. C 改为 swimming   6. B 改为 for   7. C 改为 the same
　　8. B 改为 working   9. A 改为 stolen   10. D 改为 increasing

For Better Performance

一、1. D 2. D 3. B 4. C 5. D

二、1. to be honest   2. lead to   3. agree with somebody   4. thanks to
　　5. on the same page   6. depend on   7. 二维码   8. 利和弊
　　9. 信用卡   10. 感谢   11. 对……有影响   12. 手机支付

三、1. serve   2. AI   3. mobile   4. cooked   5. enjoyable
　　6. Education   7. improve   8. apply   9. communicate   10. depends

四、1. D 改为 on   2. A 改为 for   3. A 改为 answering
　　4. B 改为 arrived in   5. A 改为 his

单元检测

第一部分　英语知识运用

第一节　1. D　2. A　3. A　4. B　5. D

第二节　6. C　7. B　8. A　9. C　10. C　11. A　12. B　13. D　14. A　15. B
16. D　17. A　18. B　19. B　20. C　21. B　22. C　23. B　24. A　25. C
26. D　27. C　28. A　29. B　30. D

第三节　31. B　32. A　33. C　34. D　35. A　36. C　37. A　38. D　39. B　40. B

第二部分　篇章与词汇理解

第一节　41. A　42. B　43. D　44. A　45. C　46. B　47. C　48. D　49. B　50. A
51. D　52. A　53. B　54. C　55. A

第二节　56. E　57. A　58. D　59. C　60. I　61. H　62. B　63. G　64. J　65. F

第三节　66. E　67. A　68. D　69. B　70. C

第三部分　语言技能运用

第一节　71. apply　72. advantages　73. perform　74. depend on　75. benefit

第二节　76. effect　77. improvement　78. addressed　79. led　80. welcoming

第三节　81. D 改为 to leave　82. A 改为 interested　83. D 改为 to eat
84. A 改为 singing　85. A 改为 amazing

第四节

AI plays an important role in our lives and it also has more advantages. But every coin has its two sides. In my opinion, AI is more a threat than an assistant. Firstly, AI is used on the assembly line which leads to many people losing their jobs. Secondly, AI robots are used in restaurants, department stores and so on, but they have no emotion. They couldn't communicate with people really like human. Thirdly, it also lacks of safety, it can cause insecurity. It can't work without electricity. At last, I am worried about that once the robot is smarter than we think. They may be unwilling to be human's serve anymore. One day the robot will replace human to be the owner of the world. So I think AI is not a good thing.

Unit 4　Customer Service

Warming-up

二、1. complaint　2. receipt　3. delay　4. delivery　5. inconvenience　6. promise

7. 掌管　负责　8. 把……修理一下　9. 投诉　10. 处理　11. 由于　12. 确保

Listening and Speaking

一、1. D　2. A　3. D　4. A　5. C

二、1. D　2. C　3. B　4. E　5. A

三、1. B　2. A　3. E　4. D　5. C

四、

A：Good afternoon！What can I do for you？

B：I'd like to have the necklace refunded.

A：What's the problem？

B：You overcharged me five hundred *yuan*.

A：Why do you say that？

B：Because my friend bought the same one last week，it only cost him 5,000 Yuan.

A：Would you please show me your receipts？

B：Certainly here you are！

A. Oh I see. Your friend bought it on our VIP Day. So it's cheaper.

B：So that's how it is. Thank you for your patience.

A：You are welcome！

Reading and Writing

一、1. charged　2. serve　3. complaint　4. patience　5. apologize

6. amazed　7. interesting　8. guarantee　9. painted　10. solution

二、1. C　2. A　3. C　4. D　5. D　6. B　7. D　8. A　9. C　10. B

三、1. B 2. D 3. A 4. C 5. B

四、

Dear Wang,

Today I'm writing to complain about the delayed delivery of my flowers for Mother's day. Last night, I ordered fresh flower from your online store which were expected to arrive before twelve o'clock this morning. However, I didn't receive them until fifteen o'clock this afternoon. I was so disappointed for your bad service. Not only were they delayed but also the flowers were faded. So I want to have them refunded and have my money back. I'm attaching here with photographs of your flowers for your reference. I hope you can check it and give me a satisfactory answer as soon as possible.

Best wishes!

Yours sincerely,
Li Ming

Grammar

一、1. B 2. C 3. A 4. B 5. D 6. A 7. A 8. B 9. C 10. A
　　11. B 12. D 13. B 14. C 15. B 16. B 17. C 18. D 19. B 20. A
　　21. B 22. D 23. C 24. A 25. C 26. B 27. C 28. D 29. C 30. C

二、1. C 改为去掉 so 2. C 改为 were 3. C 改为去掉 but 4. C 改为 finishes

　　5. B 改为 whatever 6. B 改为 had 7. A 改为 so 8. C 改为 catches

　　9. A 改为 such 10. B 改为 so that

For Better Performance

一、1. A 2. D 3. B 4. C 5. A

二、1. 起初 2. 例如 3. 决定做某事 4. 按时 5. 尽快 6. 尽某人最大努力做某事

　　7. make an apology 8. arrange to do something 9. give back 10. exchange for

　　11. under guarantee 12. make a promise

三、1. arrangement 2. delayed 3. deal with 4. result 5. unless

6. mentioned 7. loss 8. delivered 9. exchange 10. sincere

四、1. A 改为 how 2. B 改为 beginning 3. D 改为 due to 4. B 改为 so 5. B 改为 as

单元检测

第一部分 英语知识运用

第一节 1. A 2. C 3. D 4. B 5. C

第二节 6. C 7. D 8. A 9. A 10. C 11. B 12. C 13. A 14. D 15. C

16. B 17. A 18. D 19. B 20. C 21. A 22. C 23. B 24. D 25. B

26. B 27. D 28. A 29. C 30. C

第三节 31. D 32. C 33. A 34. B 35. D 36. A 37. A 38. B 39. C 40. D

第二部分 篇章与词汇理解

第一节 41. A 42. B 43. D 44. D 45. C 46. A 47. D 48. B 49. C 50. D

51. A 52. D 53. B 54. C 55. B

第二节 56. C 57. D 58. E 59. B 60. A 61. I 62. J 63. F 64. G 65. H

第三节 66. E 67. A 68. B 69. C 70. D

第三部分 语言技能运用

第一节 71. exchange 72. solution 73. patience 74. receipt 75. blanks

第二节 76. convenient 77. goods 78. complaints 79. charged 80. Check

第三节 81. C 改为 will you 82. B 改为 to 83. B 改为 have been cut

84. A 改为 Because of 85. A 改为 mentioned

第四节

Dear Li Ming,

Thank you for your trust in our shop. I'm sorry that I have made you feel unpleasant. Here I'd like to express my sincere apology to you. Now I have known all about it. Because there are too many orders, the delivery is not timely and the flowers aren't fresh, either. So I'm responsible for it. I'll pay for all your loss. I will reduce the price of the flowers by 5% which you ordered today. Beyond that, I will arrange for a second delivery of fresh flowers to you for free and make sure you're satisfied with them.

Sorry again for all the trouble and hope you will support my shop as before.

Yours faithfully,

Mike

Unit 5　Natural Wonders in the World

Warming-up

二、1. 吸引　2. 人物　3. 采访　4. 栩栩如生的;逼真的　5. 旅行社

6. destination　7. distance　8. discover　9. impressive　10. be located in

11. unique　12. according to

Listening and Speaking

一、1. B　2. A　3. B　4. A　5. B

二、1. B　2. C　3. D　4. A　5. E

三、1. A　2. D　3. E　4. C　5. B

四、

Jane：Hi, David. Where did you go during the holiday?

David：I went to Beijing with my parents.

Jane：Can you tell me something about the Great Wall?

David：Sure. It's my pleasure.

Jane：Where is it located in?

David：It is located in China.

Jane：Have you ever been there?

David：Yes, I have been there twice.

Jane：How do you like the Great Wall?

David：It is one of the world's most famous wonders. It is amazing and marvelous.

Jane：Can you say something more about it?

David：It is interesting. Thousands of travelers from all parts of the world come to visit the
　　　　Great Wall every year.

Jane: Oh! Great! I'll see the wonder myself someday.

David: Yes, it is really worth visiting.

Reading and Writing

一、1. destination   2. Distance   3. forecast   4. wonders   5. interview
　　6. impressive   7. attractive   8. discovery   9. various   10. width

二、1. B   2. A   3. D   4. C   5. C   6. A   7. D   8. B   9. C   10. B

三、1. B   2. B   3. B   4. A   5. C

四、

Mountain Tai

Mountain Tai is the first mountain in the five high mountains. It lies in the middle of Shandong Province, and in the north of Tai'an. Mountain Tai has a great momentum, the area of which is about 426 square kilometers and the top of which is about 1545 meters above sea level, so sometimes we describe a person, we also say that the person is steady like Mountain Tai. On the Mountain Tai, Buddhism and Taoism are very popular, so many emperors of the past visited it. They built temples, moulded statues, and inscribed characters on the stones, which left us many cultural objects and history spot. Some celebrities of the past also admire Mountain Tai and come to see the sights one after another, which left us many famous poems and literary works.

Grammar

一、1. D   2. C   3. D   4. A   5. D   6. C   7. B   8. C   9. D   10. D
　　11. A   12. B   13. C   14. B   15. A   16. B   17. D   18. D   19. C   20. B
　　21. D   22. D   23. B   24. C   25. B   26. B   27. C   28. B   29. A   30. B

二、1. C 改为 which   2. C 改为 I can   3. C 改为 where   4. B 改为 why
　　5. B 改为 whether   6. C 改为 had been   7. C 改为 goes   8. C 改为 is
　　9. C 改为 would   10. B 改为 that

For Better Performance

一、1. C   2. C   3. C   4. D   5. B

二、1. 自然奇观   2. 列出原因   3. 令人惊奇的   4. 旅行目的地   5. 发展成为

6. 看起来像　7. introduce…to…　8. be known as…　9. between and

10. from…to…　11. be regarded as　12. be filled with

三、1. length　2. impression　3. interviewer　4. wonderful　5. larger

6. tourists　7. towering　8. lifelike　9. border　10. represent

四、1. C 改为 that　2. A 改为 asked　3. B 改为 whether　4. B 改为 have　5. B 改为 as

单元检测

第一部分　英语知识运用

第一节　1. C　2. B　3. B　4. C　5. A

第二节　6. B　7. B　8. D　9. A　10. B　11. A　12. B　13. D　14. C　15. C

16. B　17. A　18. A　19. B　20. C　21. D　22. D　23. C　24. A　25. D

26. B　27. A　28. A　29. C　30. B

第三节　31. C　32. B　33. B　34. D　35. B　36. A　37. C　38. B　39. A　40. D

第二部分　篇章与词汇理解

第一节　41. A　42. B　43. D　44. C　45. A　46. B　47. C　48. B　49. A　50. C

51. A　52. D　53. B　54. C　55. C

第二节　56. B　57. A　58. G　59. H　60. F　61. I　62. E　63. D　64. C　65. J

第三节　66. E　67. B　68. C　69. A　70. D

第三部分　语言技能运用

第一节　71. distance　72. interview　73. invite　74. powerful　75. claimed

第二节　76. differences　77. introduction　78. located　79. unforgettable　80. beauty

第三节　81. A 改为 What　82. B 改为 interested　83. C 改为 any other

84. D 改为 the time is　85. A 改为 have never

第四节

The Imperial Mountain Summer Resort

The Imperial Mountain Summer Resort is located in the city of Chengde, is Chinese largest imperial garden, twice the size of Beijing's summer palace. The Mountain Resort is one of the four most famous Chinese gardens and one of the largest and best-preserved imperial palaces outside Beijing.

Building of the Mountain Resort began in 1703 under the rule of Emperor Kangxi and was finished in 1790 under the rule of Emperor Qianlong. The Mountain Resort was built to be a second political center apart from Beijing, for the emperor would stay here for about half a year to attend political and foreign affairs.

It is said that the Imperial Mountain Summer Resort has seen the Qing Dynasty's development and its rich history, so it is really a national and religious history museum. It's not only a famous tourist attraction in China, but also a world cultural heritage, national AAAAA tourist attraction.

Unit 6 Living History of Culture

Warming-up

二、1. 令人震惊的   2. 建设，建筑物   3. 极好的   4. ……的起点   5. 在……的边缘

   6. ancient   7. especially   8. expression   9. regular   10. grey   11. the Silk Road

   12. originally

Listening and Speaking

一、1. B   2. B   3. A   4. D   5. C

二、1. A   2. E   3. B   4. D   5. C

三、1. A   2. C   3. D   4. B   5. E

四、

Bill: Where did you go during the holiday?

Tom: I went to Dali with my friends.

Bill: Are you interested in this city?

Tom: I'm interested in it. It has a long and splendid history.

Bill: Where is Dali?

Tom: It is located in the west of Yunnan Province. It is also the capital of the Dali Bai Autonomous Prefecture.

Bill: Where did you go in Dali?

Tom：Erhai Lake，Cangshan Mountain，Dali Ancient Town and so on.

Bill：Which is the most attractive?

Tom：It must be Cangshan. It attracts thousands of tourists all over the world.

Reading and Writing

一、1. square   2. fantastic   3. grey   4. ancient   5. regular

　　6. construction   7. Amazingly   8. especially   9. expression

　　10. Originally

二、1. D   2. A   3. B   4. B   5. C   6. C   7. D   8. C   9. B   10. A

三、1. C   2. C   3. A   4. C   5. D

四、

Welcome to Beijing

Beijing is the capital of China and the nation's center for politics，economy and culture. It's the place which I've visited twice. I am interested in this city.

Beijing is an ancient city with a long history. There are numerous heritage sites and wonderful examples of ancient architecture，such as world-famous Great Wall，the Temple of Heaven and the Forbidden City. Besides sightseeing places，there are many delicious food，such as，Peking ducks and Beijing snacks.

Beijing is really a good place to travel. It attracts thousands of people every year.

Grammar

一、1. A   2. B   3. B   4. B   5. C   6. A   7. B   8. A   9. B   10. B

　　11. C   12. C   13. A   14. B   15. B   16. C   17. D   18. C   19. D   20. B

　　21. D   22. A   23. C   24. D   25. D   26. D   27. D   28. A   29. C   30. A

二、1. C 改为 whose   2. B 改为 whom   3. C 改为 that   4. C 改为 that   5. A 改为 which

　　6. C 改为 when/ on which   7. A 改为 who   8. A 改为 whether   9. B 改为 whether

　　10. B 改为 turns

For Better Performance

一、1. C   2. A   3. D   4. D   5. A

二、1. 与……相比 2. 对……感兴趣 3. 在他 30 多岁时 4. 丰盛的菜肴
5. 使某人想起 6. 由……制成 7. step into… 8. around the world
9. eating habits 10. be listed as 11. start with 12. due to

三、1. Cultural 2. exactly 3. regularly 4. stretching 5. attract
6. stretch 7. brilliant 8. attractive 9. differences 10. block

四、1. B 改为 which 2. C 改为 with 3. B 改为 on which(where) 4. C 改为 that
5. B 改为 such

单元检测

第一部分 英语知识运用

第一节 1. A 2. B 3. C 4. A 5. A

第二节 6. D 7. A 8. A 9. A 10. B 11. A 12. C 13. D 14. A 15. B
16. B 17. C 18. B 19. C 20. C 21. A 22. D 23. C 24. A 25. A
26. C 27. D 28. B 29. A 30. D

第三节 31. B 32. C 33. A 34. C 35. C 36. B 37. C 38. A 39. C 40. A

第二部分 篇章与词汇理解

第一节 41. B 42. A 43. B 44. A 45. C 46. A 47. C 48. B 49. D 50. B
51. A 52. B 53. B 54. D 55. A

第二节 56. A 57. C 58. I 59. J 60. H 61. E 62. D 63. B 64. G 65. F

第三节 66. D 67. A 68. E 69. B 70. C

第三部分 语言技能运用

第一节 71. typical 72. celebration 73. amazing 74. impression 75. history

第二节 76. introduction 77. wonderful 78. traditional 79. Attracted 80. beauty

第三节 81. B 改为 so much 82. D 改为 treasures 83. C 改为 owns 84. B 改为 doing
85. B 改为 learn about

第四节

Paper cutting

Paper cutting is one of the most popular Chinese traditional folk arts. It has a history of more than one hundred years. From the 7th to the 13th century, paper cutting became popular during

Chinese festivals. The art spread to many other countries in the 14th century. Paper cutting works are usually made of red paper. Red is the most popular color in Chinese culture.

It is easy to learn how to make paper cutting works. What we need is simply a piece of paper and a knife or a pair of scissors. But to be good at this art is not easy at all because it needs much practice and imagination.

From the art of paper cutting, people can know about Chinese culture, history and stories of people's life. It shows the wisdom and creation of Chinese people, we should try our best to make more people know about it.

Unit 7 Natural Disasters

Warming-up

二、1. 台风 2. 干旱 3. 地震 4. 洪水 5. 热浪 6. 沙尘暴 7. 酸雨 8. 交通工具
　　9. 火山 10. 城市的 11. 频繁地 12. 被迫，强迫，力量 13. 讨论
　　14. protect…from/against… 15. prevent 16. sustainable development
　　17. due to… 18. be polluted by… 19. lead to… 20. loss
　　21. make a change 22. promote 23. tie…to…

Listening and Speaking

一、1. B 2. A 3. A 4. B 5. A

二、1. B 2. A 3. C 4. E 5. D

三、1. A 2. C 3. B 4. D 5. E

四、

Mary Fisher: Hello, Chen Jie. I thought you were going to Thailand this morning.

Chen Jie: My flight is delayed due to the floods. Other public transportations like trains and
　　　　　 ships have also been canceled or delayed.

Mary Fisher: That's terrible. It seems there have been more floods these years than before.

Chen Jie: Yes. And also the typhoons, wildfire and smog.

Mary Fisher: These natural disasters have caused great damage to our life.

Chen Jie: That's certainly true. And some of them are caused by human activities.

Mary Fisher: Yes. We've burned too much coal and oil and badly polluted the environment.

Chen Jie: Well, it's lucky that people have decided to make a change.

Mary Fisher: Yes. It's what we should do right now. And the most important thing is how we can have more people join us.

Chen Jie: I agree with you. If more people work together, it'll be possible for us to protect our earth and make it a safe and lovely place to live in.

Reading and Writing

一、1. energy   2. urban   3. responsible   4. frequently   5. discussions
      6. caused   7. environmental   8. importance   9. naturally   10. Promoting

二、1. D   2. A   3. C   4. A   5. C   6. A   7. D   8. B   9. C   10. B

三、1. C   2. A   3. A   4. C   5. B

四、

Improve the environment

Good environment can make people feel happy. To improve the environment means making our life quality. What should we do to improve our environment?

We should plant more trees. And we should prevent those factories from pouring waste water into rivers, lakes and fields. Whenever we see litter on the ground, we should pick it up and throw it into a dustbin.

Don't spit in public places. Don't draw on public walls. It's our duty to keep our earth clean and tidy.

Grammar

一、1. B   2. B   3. B   4. C   5. C   6. B   7. C   8. B   9. B   10. B
    11. B   12. A   13. A   14. C   15. D   16. D   17. B   18. A   19. B   20. A
    21. D   22. A   23. D   24. B   25. B   26. A   27. B   28. A   29. B   30. B

二、1. A 改为 It   2. A 改为 Whether   3. B 改为 who   4. B 改为 that

5. B 改为 reported   6. D 改为（should）start   7. A 改为 It

8. A 改为 they held   9. A 改为 whether   10. B 改为 what

For Better Performance

一、1. C   2. D   3. D   4. A   5. B

二、1. 导致   2. 由于   3. 越来越多   4. 众所周知   5. 可持续发展

6. 对……负责   7. traffic jam   8. private cars   9. natural disasters

10. It is + adj + to do sth   11. electric cars

三、1. polluted   2. powered   3. growing   4. natural   5. to make

6. activities   7. frequently   8. public   9. canceled   10. floods

四、1. C 改为 for   2. B 改为 more frequently   3. D 改为 caused   4. D 改为 to smog

5. C 改为 changes

单元检测

第一部分   英语知识运用

第一节   1. A   2. A   3. B   4. B   5. C

第二节   6. A   7. A   8. A   9. D   10. A   11. D   12. A   13. A   14. C   15. C

16. A   17. B   18. C   19. A   20. A   21. C   22. A   23. C   24. D   25. B

26. B   27. C   28. A   29. C   30. D

第三节   31. C   32. C   33. B   34. D   35. A   36. B   37. C   38. A   39. B   40. D

第二部分   篇章与词汇理解

第一节   41. C   42. D   43. B   44. A   45. C   46. D   47. B   48. B   49. C   50. A

51. A   52. C   53. D   54. B   55. D

第二节   56. F   57. D   58. G   59. C   60. H   61. B   62. I   63. A   64. J   65. E

第三节   66. C   67. D   68. B   69. A   70. E

第三部分   语言技能运用

第一节   71. smog   72. natural   73. identify   74. protect   75. environment

第二节   76. badly   77. actions   78. reuse   79. Promoting   80. more frequently

第三节   81. A 改为 they held   82. A 改为 whether   83. B 改为 what

84. A 改为 That they   85. C 改为 that

第四节

How to Protect our Environment

In order to protect our environment, we should do the following things. First, we should plant more trees and flowers. Also, always remember not to throw rubbish or pour waste water everywhere. As we all know, water is becoming less and less. So it's quite necessary to save water. For example, turn the tap off after washing. Last but not least, we'd better ride a bike or walk when going out instead of driving a car. In my opinion, if everyone tries his best to protect the environment, our city will become nicer and cleaner.

Unit 8　Role Models of the Times

Warming-up

二、1. 英雄　2. championship　3. 运动员　4. firefighter　5. 科学家　6. safe

　　7. 为……做贡献　8. admire　9. 把……奉献于　10. respectable

Listening and Speaking

一、1. C　2. B　3. D　4. C　5. A

二、1. C　2. E　3. D　4. B　5. A

三、1. D　2. B　3. A　4. E　5. C

四、

Zhang Li: Hi, Yang Juan. What are you reading?

Yang Juan: I'm reading a piece of news about Zhang Guimei, who was presented with the title "Role Model of the times".

Zhang Li: Oh, really? I have never heard of her. Who is she?

Yang Juan: She is the headmaster of a high school for girls from poor families. She devoted most of her time and money to her students.

Zhang Li: What a respectable person she is!

Yang Juan: You're right. And she is my role model.

Zhang Li: She is also the kind of person I respect. I'd like to be a teacher like her.

Yang Juan：We have the same dream.

Reading and Writing

一、1. achievement   2. malaria   3. contribute   4. award   5. discovery

6. medal   7. treatment   8. region   9. Undoubtedly   10. Hybrid

二、1. A   2. B   3. C   4. D   5. B   6. A   7. C   8. D   9. A   10. B

三、1. C   2. B   3. A   4. D   5. B

四、

My Role Model

<u>Role models make a difference to us.</u> My mother is my role model.

My mother is hard-working. Every day she gets up very early and goes to bed late. She is not only busy with her work but also takes good care of my sister and me. She has made important contributions to our family. What's more, my mother is very helpful. When our neighbors have some difficulty, she's always ready to help them.

I'm so lucky to have such a good mother. I love her and I will learn from her. She makes me know the importance of diligence and kindness. I will study hard and try my best to help others.

Grammar

一、1. C   2. B   3. A   4. D   5. B   6. A   7. D   8. C   9. B   10. D
   11. A   12. C   13. B   14. D   15. A   16. C   17. B   18. A   19. C   20. B
   21. D   22. A   23. B   24. D   25. C   26. A   27. D   28. A   29. C   30. B

二、1. Hearing the news   2. Having returned   3. Walking   4. to catch   5. old enough to

6. Being ill   7. strong, to   8. Born   9. Not knowing   10. for; to see

For Better Performance

一、1. A   2. C   3. D   4. B   5. C

二、1. 奖励，授予   2. essential   3. 发现   4. glory   5. 领头位置，榜样

6. medal   7. 尊敬，敬仰   8. respectable   9. 成功（做某事）   10. role model

三、1. admire   2. contributions   3. prize   4. professional   5. respectable

6. champion   7. essential   8. firefighters   9. standard   10. model

四、1. A 改为 safe   2. C 改为 models   3. D 改为 grow   4. C 改为 putting

— 23 —

5. D 改为 countries

单元检测

第一部分　英语知识运用

第一节　1. B　2. C　3. A　4. D　5. C

第二节　6. D　7. A　8. B　9. C　10. A　11. B　12. D　13. C　14. D　15. A
16. B　17. C　18. D　19. A　20. C　21. B　22. D　23. A　24. C　25. B
26. C　27. A　28. D　29. B　30. C

第三节　31. C　32. B　3. A　34. C　35. A　36. D　37. B　38. D　39. C　40. A

第二部分　篇章与词汇理解

第一节　A篇：41. A　42. B　43. D　44. C　45. A
B篇：46. B　47. D　48. D　49. C　50. A
C篇：51. C　52. A　53. C　54. D　55. B

第二节　56. I　57. E　58. J　59. B　60. A　61. G　62. C　63. D　64. F　65. H

第三节　66. D　67. A　68. C　69. E　70. B

第三部分　语言技能运用

第一节　71. firefighter　72. medal　73. treatment　74. admire　75. standard

第二节　76. contributions　77. achievement　78. discoveries　79. player　80. professional

第三节　81. C 改为 to win　82. A 改为 to　83. D 改为 contribute to
84. B 改为 deliberately　85. D 改为 as

第四节

The Hero in My Heart

<u>Heroes have a great influence on our life.</u> The hero in my heart is Zhang Guimei.

Zhang Guimei used to be a teacher. She taught Chinese and politics. She worked hard though she was ill. She was strict and worked to high standards. She always had a heart full of love. She cared about the students' daily life and helped them with their schoolwork. She tried her best to stop girls dropping out of school. She devoted her life to her students. She has impressed me with her spirit. I want to be an excellent teacher like her.